Tiffini's beautiful words come from a tender place of understanding mixed with the kind of gritty strength we all need for our broken places. *Misfit Table* will help you believe, more than ever, that you can find true acceptance, healing, and redemption for your hurt by allowing God to rewrite your story.

Lysa TerKeurst, #1 *New York Times* bestselling
author, president of Proverbs 31 Ministries

In *Misfit Table*, Tiffini weaves a story that is both spellbinding and majestic. It is the telling of the ultimate love story of a faithful God who never stops his pursuit of our hearts. Read and discover God's love, his goodness, and how a relationship with him can redeem even the most broken fragments of our lives.

Lisa Bevere, *New York Times* bestselling author

All of us have lived under lies —those hurtful words that drape over us like a heavy blanket, words the enemy uses to keep us in bondage— but those words were labels we were never created to wear. I believe this book will be a lifeline of freedom for so many. Thank you, Tiffani, for telling your story. Your vulnerability reminds us all that we are wanted and valued, and that we always have a seat at his table.

Natalie Grant, singer/songwriter

In this world that values perfection, or at least the appearance of it, God looks for brokenness. He waits for people who chase after him, even if they do it with a limp. Tiffini is my friend. I have known few people who have embraced the process of brokenness with obedience, worship, and thanksgiving like Tiffini.

Niles Holsinger, pastor of Gateway Church

Misfit Table left me so deeply encouraged and even surprised all over again by the great lengths the Father will go to in inviting us to his table, over and over again. Tiffini so bravely and beautifully lays her heart out on the table to help all of us misfits remember that the Word of God still keeps us, heals us, and deeply satisfies our every need!

Christy Nockels, worship leader, songwriter, creator of *The Glorious in the Mundane*

I couldn't put *Misfit Table* down! The deep hurt and vulnerability of Tiffini's life story being covered so completely with the words from Papa God was soul-lifting in a way I can't fully describe. This book is a beautiful reminder that God's never-ending love for us is far greater than the brokenness of this world. His promises are true and good. His love never fails.

Korie Robertson, *Duck Dynasty*, author of *Strong and Kind*

Tiffini speaks to all who crave belonging, to be fully known and fully loved. I am forever marked by her bravery on these pages; she speaks what many yearn to say. There is no one beyond God's love, no misfit beyond his reach. May her redemption story call your heart home, as it did for mine.

Rebekah Lyons, author of *You are Free* and *Freefall to Fly*

Misfit Table will not only keep you captivated as you read through Tiffani's beautifully written words but will show you the way home. If your life has been filled with overwhelming heartache, loss, rejection, and pain, Tiffini shows you that there is a Father in heaven who has never left you nor forsaken you. He has been there the whole time, leaving "breadcrumbs," as she calls them, to lead you home.

Alex Seeley, lead pastor of The Belonging Co., author of *Tailor Made*

I can say about *Misfit Table* what I can say about only a rare few books: it captured me early and kept me until the end. It made me hungry for Jesus, whose story Tiffini really tells. Gorgeous, gripping word pictures paint an honest offering in book pages I won't soon forget.

Lisa Whittle, speaker, author of *I Want God* and *5-Word Prayers* podcast

As a therapist, I find that the balance of the clinical and the spiritual is such a fine line. Tiffini does an amazing job of understanding the truth of what she faced in her story while also hearing the raw and honest words from the Father. Such a great book for anyone who has experienced any struggle, at any time. She demonstrates, with such grace, how to lean into the Father while tending to her own tangible emotion. I cannot wait to use this with clients in my practice!

Cassie Reid, PhD; LPC-Supervisor; director of counseling at The King's University; owner/ lead therapist at Cassie Reid Counseling

Tiffini has pulled back the curtain of religion and invited us into real, raw, authentic relationship with others and with God. The reality is that Tiffini's story is all too common yet untold in the people you sit next to at church or on public transport or even at your table.

Most don't have the courage or platform to tell their story in such a way that it brings God's healing, love, and relationship. I can feel Tiffini's and God's heartbeat for each other and for the readers.

Mary Jo Pierce, author, speaker, intercessor

Tiffini's brilliant words in *Misfit Table* are everything our hurting world desperately needs. What makes this book so powerful is that these words have been lived out by an incredible author who we gratefully get to call a friend. The Bible informs us that the power of life and death resides in our words, which is why you need all the words written in this book. They will inspire you to live out your God-given design with joy and confidence.

Chris Durso, author of *Misfit* and *The Heist*

Tiffini's story will take you on a journey that will encourage you, shock you, make you mad, break your heart, and bring you hope. Each step will lead you into the arms of a loving Father, or Papa as Tiffini calls him. *Misfit Table* is an invitation for all who are hungry, an altar for the broken, and a must-read for those longing for the church to be more than a building.

Caleb Peavy, founder of Unmutable,
host of the *Be Creative* podcast

Tiffini Kilgore is a woman who knows how to use her words. She is a woman who believes with every fiber of her being that words matter, and she wields them accordingly. This book is living proof.

Jeremy Cowart, photographer,
founder of The Purpose Hotel

Misfit
TABLE

Misfit
TABLE

Let Your Hunger Lead You
to Where You Belong

By Tiffini Kilgore

ZONDERVAN

Misfit Table
Copyright © 2019 by Tiffini Kilgore

Requests for information should be addressed to:
Zondervan, *3900 Sparks Dr. SE, Grand Rapids, Michigan 49546*

ISBN 978-0-310-35149-8 (hardcover)

ISBN 978-0-310-35775-9 (audio)

ISBN 978-0-310-35234-1 (ebook)

All Scripture quotations, unless otherwise indicated, are taken from The Holy Bible, New International Version®, NIV®. Copyright © 1973, 1978, 1984, 2011 by Biblica, Inc.® Used by permission of Zondervan. All rights reserved worldwide. www.Zondervan.com. The "NIV" and "New International Version" are trademarks registered in the United States Patent and Trademark Office by Biblica, Inc.®

Scripture quotations marked MSG are from *The Message.* Copyright © 1993, 1994, 1995, 1996, 2000, 2001, 2002 by Eugene H. Peterson. Used by permission of NavPress. All rights reserved. Represented by Tyndale House Publishers, Inc.

Any internet addresses (websites, blogs, etc.) and telephone numbers in this book are offered as a resource. They are not intended in any way to be or imply an endorsement by Zondervan, nor does Zondervan vouch for the content of these sites and numbers for the life of this book.

Some names and identifying details have been changed to protect the privacy of individuals mentioned in this work.

The author is represented by The Christopher Ferebee Agency, www.christopherferebee.com.

Art direction and cover photo: Micah Kandros
Interior design: Kait Lamphere and Denise Froehlich

Printed in the United States of America

19 20 21 22 23 24 25 26 27 28 29 /LSC/ 15 14 13 12 11 10 9 8 7 6 5 4 3 2 1

For Jesus, to whom I belong
My first love, my true home

Contents

Acknowledgments

Jesus, not one page of this book could have been written or lived without you. It's your story of rescue. My story of letting you. It's a book about pain and how the true gospel is the only medicine and food for hurting and hungry hearts. Pain doesn't need numbing; it needs the gospel of put back togetherness, accompanied with sides of safety, family (blood or not), home, and help. You're what we all are needful of, really.

I've wrestled with this acknowledgment until the ninth hour. The daunting task of listing the names of everyone I've ever known so as to not hurt anyone shuts me down. So here is what I decided: to mention the two people that without them, my God-story would never have been known—known to myself first, then to you, the readers.

To the two friends, Seth and Stephanie, for editing my words down so you wouldn't have a 500,000-page book to read (who would read that?) and who risked asking for the story behind House of Belonging. This book would not be alive and neither would I, really, without you helping me carry the weight of my pain to the cross and helping me put words on it. I don't think you know how deeply grateful, even wordless (and that's *big*), I am that you helped me. You have always been for me. And you never left me in the process. Fear is contagious but so is hope. Thank you for giving me hope.

To Jana, for finding me and never letting me go.

To the team at Zondervan, I'm truly humbled by everyone. Each of you have been full of grace for me and the message of *Misfit Table*. Stephanie, Alicia, Kim, Andrea, Curt, Kait, and everyone else, thank you!

To my family, especially Nikki, Chelsee, Reece, Dakota, and Grace. I give you my little. Always. My prayer is that all the things God put in my heart are more for you than me—keep running with them. This is a new beginning. Let's let God's gospel of put back togetherness grab us and never let go.

The Beginning

This weightless warmth, this amniotic fluid, is my home within a home within a home, and outside, people walk and talk, unaware that their sounds penetrate, that I can feel.

My cells absorb sounds like sponges. My arms and legs, my hands and feet, my brain, all of me is shaped by my mother's emotional chemical rushes. My heart has roots drawing up. I am knit together as words spat by my father in anger hijack my mother's hormones, sending a wash of fight-or-flight chemicals through her body, through mine. She is afraid.

I thrash from side to side, then suck my thumb. Soothed, I quiet myself and sleep.

I do not know what kind of world I will enter next. In just a short window of time, I will be forced from my home. I'll come out writhing and wild, swimming from blood-stained water into the arms of trauma. I'll be under the influence of drugs even as the water and blood and chemicals of my mother's lineage course through me.

I will be naked as first creation and armored as Eve after the fall. I will be named.

Papa comes, catches me. His hands gently bring my hands from a flailing hallelujah, tucking them together in tiny prayer, quieting me, having moved from union with my mother into painful separation.

He gazes into my eyes as he swaddles me with his words, marking me with his love, ushering me to sleep in heavenly peace, even as I am brand-new to this earth. He lifts me, whispering, "Little one, there is something like the instinct of a tiny bird living inside you. It aches always for home. It is a homing device meant to lead you back to Papa. Listen and follow the sound."

Offering

At age eight, I can't read between the lines, but I can feel them. I sense the unspoken things.

I ask my mom for cereal in the mornings, but she never seems to hear me. My dad—where is he? There are unspoken messages everywhere, a script everyone seems to know. In that script no one pays attention to Tiffini. In that script my role has few lines. In that script I am cast an orphan. Only an observer.

Somehow, my little heart knows how to read the pressure and temperature of places. It's cold in the house, in my room. Everything bears down. All the fear, all the distraction, all of everyone's pain. I can see behind people's eyes too. There is no life in them—not in Mom's or Norman's or the lady's from the bar with hair the color of a raven's he brought home that changed everything. There's no life in any of it.

Sitting on my bed I line up my dolls. Tell them I want to put Norman and Mom back together again. I don't understand why that lady came. Why Mom doesn't like it. I want to tell the sadness to leave. I want the emptiness that feels like hungry, to be full. I want language I can understand. Eyes that can read closed doors. Rooms that don't feel thick, dark, and cold.

I tell my dolls that when I grow up I want to be a mommy. Teach school. Maybe I can teach how to keep mommies and daddies together. Maybe if they stayed together, I would too.

Norman, my stepdad, is the closest thing to a father I have. He looks like the photos of Elvis I've seen—a hunk of burning love looking for trouble. And he plays in a band—Stormin' Norman and the KC Three. Mom said she met him at a bar, and soon after, she taught herself how to play guitar. She sneaked into his world through its back door.

Sometimes, we make believe we're different people. Norman pretends he is a rock and roll star. Mom pretends she is his groupie. I pretend I am wealthy, that I can afford to buy a new guitar for Norman and a dress for my mother. My grandma pretends she's my mom, and she takes my sister and me to buy Christmas presents for my mom and Norman at JCPenney. I find a silver necklace, a silhouette of a man and woman hugging. All at once I know what I can do to make Norman stay. It costs me everything I have.

At home I pull out a piece of notebook paper and scribble a note to Norman in my best penmanship. It's as if I'm taking words from my heart and piecing them together on paper just so. I lay my broken feelings down on the cotton pad, fold up the letter, and slip it into the box. I walk slowly down the hallway. This letter is a piece of me, and my heart pounds louder and louder until it reaches my ears. All I hear is my heart beating when I tap him on the arm.

"Norman?"

As he turns and looks down, I see two me's. One wanting to run, the other standing there with a small white box cupped in two sweaty hands containing my whole heart, lifted high.

It is an offering.

I watch as he opens the envelope and reads, his eyes moving back and forth following the words. I can't hear any sound coming out of Norman's mouth, but I can feel the words gathering in my own.

This is all I have, this piece of me.

Please don't break it.

He's not hugging me or crying.

Is he thinking, "That's weird, kid"? Is his face twisting in disgust? Is he about to say, "You're not even mine."

I want to put all those words back into my heart where they came from, but I can't. He looks down, then back at the letter. The truth comes like last week when I was the last one picked at recess, and suddenly I know. Norman won't stay. Is this what Mom meant when she screamed at him the other night, calling him a cheater and unfaithful, while I was in the other room?

Norman looks at me, and though he doesn't say it, I hear him.

Your mom sucks the life out of me. She smothers me with her needs and wants and throws you kids on top of it, and I just can't handle it anymore.

I run from the room, find my mother. I'm crying now, and she stands back, feet away. She doesn't lean down, doesn't hug me or kiss me or tell me it will be okay. In her silence, though, I hear her saying, *I am the center of my world. I am full of my own needs. I need a man to be whole, and I'll have that, no matter whom I have to hurt to get it. Even you.*

21

Day after day, my mom and Norman fire messages at each other like bullets. Day after day, I try to send my own messages like love notes folded up like paper airplanes.

They don't hear me though. Maybe it's because I want everything they don't.

God, please let Norman stay . . .

Sometimes, in the quiet, I sense a message coming back to me though. A coming of heaven, of love. The pressure lifts. The room warms. I know it is Papa, the one I hear about from Grandma. He sends messages too. He crouches down, entering into my pain. Leaning in, he speaks.

Let Papa help you. Let me take your little white box, all you have to offer. Let me step in front of you so nobody can see you, so I can tend to your naked heart, your wounds. Little one, you can trust me. Let me be the One who stays and stands up for you when no one else will. Remember, Jesus could have called out to thousands of angels to rescue him off the cross. *But he stayed.* I stay because I made a way for you to come back home. I gave everything to get my family back. To get you back. You are the apple of Papa's eye.

I am everywhere and right here, little one. Some days you will feel these words, real as the sun on your skin. Other days you might not, but I'm still here. I still love you.

Little one, you can
trust me. Let me
be the one who
stays and stands
up for you when
no one else will.
—Papa

Invisible

Y ou're going to live with your dad and stepmom."
My mom says this before a giant invisible hand reaches down my throat and strangles me, telling me to shut up.

I gasp for air; I can't exhale. I can't breathe. I can't say anything. Panic dumps my thoughts out like marbles. They hit the floor, rolling in every direction. I watch one roll under the refrigerator. Gone.

Why am I going to live with Dad and my stepmom? Is there no room for me here? Why is this happening again?

"Am I talking to myself?" I say, finding my voice, but no one hears me.

Stop, stop, stop, I repeat, this time in my head. But I can't stop the questions from coming again.

"What did I do to be sent away?"

Shut up, shut up, shut up, I repeat silently, this time with more force. Asking these questions only makes it worse—the breathing, the panic, the shaking.

I feel vomit coming, but I gulp it back. The room begins turning upside down, and I feel as if its contents are being emptied out. I'm trying my best to understand, to connect the unconnectable dots.

Did you give them permission to take me? Can I change your mind, Mommy?

She doesn't answer, doesn't hear my soundless cries for help. Now I realize it. I am the contents of the room. I am the pieces being emptied out. I am not wanted here.

I wish I had hands to put over my thoughts so I can't hear them. Can't feel how they hurt.

Heat spikes up my spine and into my head, and everything throbs. My neck has a heartbeat. My blood runs like a river wild down deep in me, over my ribs, around my heart. I can't find my breath again. I can't find my voice.

The words push against my insides or maybe hold me down or maybe slam me inside a shut and locked door. I clench my hands into fists. Can I clench so hard I break bones? Can I somehow make someone come to me, maybe stop the room from closing in? No one comes, so I press my clenched fists into my eyes. I don't want to see my smallness. See their bigness. Everything closes in. Everything goes dark.

I am tired from fighting to stay, and I am only eight. I am disoriented from all the circles I have been running in.

I am out of breath from all this running, suffocating, and I am so small.

Can you not see me turning blue, Mommy? Can anybody?

Right now, I just want my grandma. Someone safe.

Please don't make me leave, Mommy. . . . I want Grandma.

My feelings, seasick. I am a boat in a violent storm. My feelings careen from side to side. I fight back the only way I know how—by closing my eyes. Pretending I am somewhere else. Anywhere but here.

I am picking you up, little one. Breathe. I am here in your now. My breath sustains every living thing, including you.

I am putting my hands under your heart, lifting it above the darkness into my marvelous light. Feel my deep wholeness stabilizing your heart. Feel the gentle rhythm of my rest.

You are big inside Papa's bigness. You are no little thing. I don't pass by, glance at you, and keep going. I kneel down, bending to your suffering.

You don't know it now, but you will. I am under your skin and in your bones. I am never away. I am always close. Always bent low.

That's my girl. Climb up in my hands. Let me warm your heart. My hands are keeping your pieces all together. I am taking you somewhere. My words are bringing your heart back.

No matter how circumstances spin you, I am your finding place. Always. I am your direction. I am true north.

chapter

three

Story

I t is a broken year, a year that's seen me shuffled around, a year that's shattered my little heart.

But I spend the months that somehow make it whole in an ornate stone church on warm sunny Sunday mornings. Grandview Baptist Church has a red carpet aisle that ends where the preacher stands. Behind him is a spacious choir alcove. The music begins playing, calling me. Invisible hands reach in and pull out melodies, and *whoosh*, I am soaring like a wild bird let out of a cage, a bird cooped up for way too long. The pieces of my heart lift into this story of song, a song that promises it can put my heart back together.

I want to be a part of this song, part of this story.

I step from the back-row pew and into the aisle. I feel very small standing at the end of the red carpet, looking up, but somehow it's as if I'm very big all at the same time. How have I found my way onto this red carpet? Red carpets are for somebodies. Moments before, I was invisible. Nobody saw me standing there between the shaming eyes of my stepmom and my sleeping dad, whose head was slumped against his chest. Nobody but God, who asked whether I'd like to join his family. I said yes to God. I said yes, I will follow you, Jesus. I said, I'll even step onto that carpet. I took his hand like a bride.

It was then that I knew. I had a home, and it wasn't here with all these people singing these songs as if they were bored. It was somewhere out there, somewhere with Jesus.

I make my way down the aisle, take the tiny white box out of the pocket of my heart—the one I tried to give to Norman—and I carry it all the way to the end of that red carpet aisle. I don't place it in the hands of the preacher. I place it on the wings of that song, and I watch it soar into the hands of God. He opens the box, finds every single piece of my heart, and he puts it back together. He gives it back to me, whole, and I smile while the choir sings to me. My tears fall, every emotion naked and exposed for all to see.

I want to follow more than be hollow. I want something to stop the ache inside. Standing at the end of that red carpet aisle, something covers me and pulls me up into a gentle hug.

God bends down and whispers, tells me I never really wanted Norman or any other father, even though I didn't realize it. He tells me I wanted him. He is different. He will stay. He can hear my heartbeat in a way nobody else has or ever can.

At night, I climb into the bottom bunk and close my eyes. I hold God's hand like I hold Grandma's hand when I sleep at her house. I'm afraid, lying in my bottom bunk alone. It's dark, and when it's dark the voices in my head talk louder and faster. Grandma knows the fear of a little girl, so maybe God does too.

God's here, holding my hand as I drift off to sleep. I know what home is. It's a song, a hug, and a lap. It's a safe house, even among lifeless people. For the first time, I'm not afraid to tell the truth. I know it now—from now on, every night, I will climb up into his lap and unpack my day or hold his hand as I go to sleep. He will pull me close while I cry uncontrollably; he'll be my home. How do I know this? I don't know. But I do.

Drifting to sleep, I recite the prayer Grandma and I prayed:

Now I lay me down to sleep,
I pray the Lord my soul to keep,
If I should die before I wake,
I pray the Lord my soul to take.

This prayer makes me feel safe and afraid all at the same time, but sensing Papa's hug in those words, I pray it all the same.

Listen to my lullaby, little one. Hear me sing. I am perfect peace. I've been holding you since before you were born. I caught you the day you entered the world, and I am catching you still. Listen to the music, this lullaby. It's gospel set to music.

I take shattered things and make them usable.
I see the end result of each crucible.
Through it all I prove my love is capable.

29

I take your broken heart and make it whole,
leading it through my love.

I make all things new, little one. My plans are good for you.
I will trade every wound, like a piece of ash, for a piece of beauty.
A beautiful legacy, an anthem that my love goes on and on.

I caught you the day you

entered the world, and I am

catching

you still.

–Papa

chapter

four

Missing Things

It's been months since I first met God, and sometimes I still feel him here. Sometimes during the day, though, the pressure is just too much.

Grandma catches me with my hands down my pants. I had wanted to turn off the noise in my body. This always seemed to do the trick.

"What are you doing?" she asks, her voice like scissors cutting the silence. What am I doing? I don't know. Whatever it is, it must be horrible the way Grandma's voice sounds gruff like she is red-faced. But how did she catch me? She isn't even looking at me; she is cooking her family recipe, tacos and enchiladas.

I read between the lines again, hear what's beneath Grandma's words.

What you're doing is naughty and doesn't belong in my house.

I want to disappear, but my cheeks are reddening, and I feel like they're glowing. Can't she see me glowing?

She continues cooking dinner, knowing that she's shamed me into stopping whatever it was I wasn't supposed to be doing. When she finishes stirring the pot, she sits in her chair, which is the color of a carrot picked fresh out of the garden and smells of smoke and old Estee Lauder. I watch her feet kick back and forth as she rocks and lights a cigarette. I begin to cry.

"Come here, baby doll, sit in my lap," she says.

"Grandma! I feel stupid. I'm too big to be rocked like a baby."

"No, you're not," she says, and she opens her arms as I climb up.

I curl up all too big as she rocks me, and tears come for all the missing things I can't name. She holds me and rocks me, and that holding and rocking keeps me together somehow. There is nothing I can do that would make her love me any less. Not even things hidden behind couch cushions. Grandma tells me this, and she tells me God is the same way. He sees all the parts of me, all the things I do, and he loves me still.

My favorite thing about Grandma, other than when she's in the kitchen cooking, is the way she talks to me about God. I don't see her talking like that to anybody else. I've never seen Grandma go to church. I don't know how she knows about God, but she does.

Grandma is all I have, really. She is old, and I sense this for the first time. I cry for when she will no longer be here. I feel it already. Her missing. She already goes missing every night around dinner time.

She keeps it under the sink—the whiskey. Dinner is the green light to begin drinking. She usually opens the bottom kitchen cabinet and pulls out the whiskey, then the grapefruit juice, in a burgundy can, from the refrigerator. She mixes it in the kitchen, just feet away from that old chair, and I always smell it—that sweet, sour, and citrus odor.

I watch her every night as she turns from Grandma into a scary person that slurs her words, and I want to tell her to let this night be different. I always want to tell her how I hate her drinking, how she can't be my grandma if she won't quit. It terrifies me when you drink, I want to say. The sounds you make after you take a drink, the smacking of your lips, I hear it every single night, and I want to drop my skin and run, I want to say. But I know I won't say it tonight. Instead, I will pretend she is the same, even though she's not. But I don't play pretend good.

While she rocks, I pretend to tell Grandma that I don't want her to turn into someone else, that I need her. If she heard my words, I think her heart would arrest. She doesn't want to feel my pain, so I keep my thoughts secret. She gets up. In that moment, I go under.

And take all of my unsaid words with me.

Grandma goes to the kitchen. I hear the creak of the cabinet, the crack of the refrigerator. I smell those sickly-sweet aromas trickling into the room. Is this what happens when you don't deserve good things? Why don't I deserve one day of complete love and attention? Do I only deserve for my heart to be a punching bag for other people? Do I only deserve a little love? Do I only deserve to be set aside? Whiskey keeps Grandma's emotions asleep, but mine are wide-awake.

Sensing Papa's soft blanket of safety, I snuggle down deep, letting him soothe me. This is my safe home, and it's like womb-love, with the pulsing of amniotic fluid, rhythmic and warm.

Hush, little one, don't you cry. Papa is singing you a lullaby.
Hush, little girl, don't you cry. Papa is writing your story line.

Let me pull you up into my lap. My hands are safe hands. Let me be your safe and soft blanket. Let me be your person. I am always safe. I won't shape-shift on you at the end of the day. I will always give you a warm lap.

Little one, I see you. You don't have to pretend. You don't have to be something you're not. You don't earn my love by shape-shifting, and you don't have to beg for my love. I am already here, delighted to be with you just as you are. I want to comfort you when the noise in your body seems too much.

Little one, you are not created to do life alone. I am hiding you in my holiness, sheltering you in my secret place, covering you in my covenant love. Let me come with you. My hands are even now smoothing out the rough places on the road we travel. I will never turn my back on you. I will not cut you off. I will never leave. No matter what you do, I am not going anywhere. Ever.

five

Tell Me I'm Okay

Grandma and I watch *I Love Lucy*. Ricky and Lucy remind me of Grandma and Grandpa. They sleep in separate beds. Grandma and Grandpa sleep in separate rooms. Tonight, I choose Grandpa's. He has two twin beds.

In the morning, I wake up and Grandpa is lying on the floor. I'm not sure why, but I am scared to touch him. His skin is gray, his eyes are open already, looking up at the ceiling. I hop off the bed and step over his body to get to Grandma's bedroom, like he might wake up and grab my feet, catching me sneaking up on Grandma sleeping.

I sneak into Grandma's room, staring at her for a moment before tapping her on the shoulder. I'm afraid to wake her, not wanting to scare her.

"Grandma," I whisper.

She jumps, wide-awake.

"What?"

"Grandpa is on the floor," I say. "I think something is wrong."

The covers catch her feet, trapping her, and she fights to get out of the bed.

Grandma taps her carton of menthol cigarettes, sliding one out like a candy bar from a vending machine. She lights it, drags deep, as if this cigarette is the last checkbox on her to-do list, and watches the ambulance people wheel Grandpa out the front door. Eyes closed. He'll never see my face again. This is our goodbye.

Grandma gets drunk early today. She slurs scary words, says Grandpa's spirit had already left his body when I found him on the floor, that he is in heaven now, and that tomorrow we will clean out his room. Everything feels like death. I do not feel safe. I am alone, waffling in dead things, whiskey, and reality. I stare at the three-year-old picture of me, smiling with the other faces, the family and friends frozen on the wall. I wish someone could come off the wall and help us, could pull us out of the dying, out of the drinking.

It's now night, and I sleep with Grandma, tucking the sheets around me so my skin won't touch hers. I don't want to smell her stale alcohol snores or feel her empty skin. I want her to wake up, roll over, and look at me. I want her to see me. I wish she'd tell me what happened to Grandpa. Tell me what death is. I want to say, tell me I'm okay and that you're okay too.

Instead, the sun takes Grandma and me down with it, and I pretend the sheets are blindfolds and that death can't find me.

I'm wide-awake, little one. I never sleep. I always listen. I do more than tell. I show and tell. I have a special place in my heart for unspoken words. I will tuck you in, safe, whispering over your heart, "You're safe, little one." Your heart is okay. I see you in the missing things. When Grandma goes missing, even when you feel you're missing, I am not missing. I'm here, and I'm not going anywhere. I am in the dark night watches.

Grandpa's Notepads

Morning comes, and I walk into Grandpa's room before my aunt and Mom come to clean out the room. I sit on the bed I was in when I noticed my dead grandpa lying on the floor. I imagine him still there, and I almost hear him say, "I have the devil sitting on my shoulder; can you see him?" He told me that on a Sunday drive with Grandma, me sitting in the back seat of their white Chevy Caprice Classic. I didn't know scary shadows had a name.

I don't know how to answer you, Grandpa.

From the bed, I see the closet, feel its magnetic pull.

Is he there? Grandpa? Now that you aren't here, your closet feels haunted. It's cluttered with gadgets, hanging white T-shirts, and skeletons. I've seen the stack of papers many times while sitting on my bed watching you get ready, pulling on your white T-shirt, tucking it tight into your trousers, slipping the belt in each loop like the hand of a clock making its way around.

Sitting on the bed, I look through a crack in the closet door and see the stacks of yellow legal pads on the shelf, and my sense of wonder stands me on my feet in front of the scary closet. Something in that closet feels bigger than me, maybe Grandpa's ghost? Grandma's told me that Yahooti and Heehaw (imaginary creatures) would get me if I went into that closet without asking, but I want something so badly that not even Yahooti or Heehaw or the devil can scare me away.

I walk into the closet, stretch on my tiptoes, grab what I can, and yank so hard I slip, sending the notepads careening into a helter-skelter pile at my feet.

I bend down and pull one up from the pile. *It is your handwriting, Grandpa, so hard to read.* It's cursive but not like what I learned in school.

Why did I see it while nobody else seemed to care it was in here?

I am holding something real but not finished. Something unread. I knew nothing about Grandpa's writings, and apparently, neither did anyone else. There are thousands of words with no ending, all left like a clue that finds me between the living and dead. Time has passed into my hands, and it feels like I am holding the world here in this moment—maybe his world, maybe my world.

I hear voices coming from the living room, so I rush another goodbye to Grandpa and rub my hand over the words like I can touch him. I scramble up on tippy-toe to push those pads back up onto the shelf to rest where I had unburied them.

Papa's presence is waking even as Grandpa's body sleeps and returns to some patch of earth. Grandpa is dead, but I have held a still living piece of him, something unfinished.

Little one, you are holding more than notebooks and memories. You are holding a story. I made you to ache for story. I made you to feel it deep and wide, like I do. I am the story.

I opened your heart to see the notebooks. The gift of words.

You are wide-awake, little one, and I know that what you're holding in your hands is why you were born. Because I put it inside you. Little one, remember the instinct of a tiny bird living inside you? I am dropping breadcrumbs that will lead you to that something-more. It sparks the fire in you aching for home. This is where you come alive, little one. Inside the words. Even though you don't know it yet. Follow them.

chapter

seven

The First Breadcrumb

It is the summer between seventh and eighth grade, and I am staying with my aunt and uncle because nobody knows what to do with me. But the storybooks do.

Books found me at school in Mrs. Hanks second grade class. If we listened and were good, we would get thirty minutes at the end of the day to read. It was like the weight of my little world would lift when I tried to control my feet to walk, not run, to the library to pick out a book.

I love the smell of books. Antiquity in a bottle. I inhale it while I wait for the librarian to stamp my card. I sit at my desk, and when I open the book, the whole room disappears. Books are where words connect one after the other after the other and I can follow them into other worlds where adventure calls to boys and girls who are brave, their voices loud.

Weeks ago, I found my aunt's stack of paperbacks while baby-sitting. I happened upon her collection of well-worn romance novels, women swooning in the arms of men on the covers. Now I spend the days crushing books, then swallowing them. I can't get enough, can't read fast enough. I down one after the other until I am light and I can breathe in this space. Someone else's words draw pictures in my mind about things men and women do. A happily-ever-after ending and those romantic feelings trigger the same feelings as when I hid behind couch cushions. Now instead of hiding, I read myself into the woman's character, imagining myself as her. I numb my reality with romance. I get lost in stories of rescue, dreaming that this will one day be me.

These books, they are not for me, but words are magnets, hands reaching out and touching me, grabbing me, yanking me in. These stories blur the lines between rescuer and captor, romance and ownership. It confuses me, yet I am drawn into its universe.

Why does reading feel safe? It doesn't hurt anyone to read these stories, and I escape my pain, my lostness. I can hide behind heroes and scenarios. I can escape into dreams.

Curled up in my chair like a cat napping in the sun, I am fixated on page seventeen when the smell of cedar and spice snaps me instantly to Grandpa's closet of white shirts and piles of unfinished legal pads, still undetected. I am not sure where Grandpa went, but he left me clues. I beg memory to remind me: Why do words call to me? What is this that I pine for?

The silence in my head scares me, with all the thoughts, feelings, and memories running around traumatized, with no words for the feelings. Maybe I need therapy to help give me the words to tell somebody what hurts. But how can I when I don't know how to put words to my feelings? The wordless sound slips out, disorderly and loud, but I'm too old to cry like a baby, so I start hiding the "sadness," mothering myself. Somehow, Grandpa's notepads tell me that if I could find the words to the something-more, they would satisfy me.

It's like these stacks of books and the notepads in Grandpa's closet have a secret they don't want to give up. But what if I ask the right questions?

I ask, and I ask, and I ask, and in my asking, it appears. The answer.

I want to write a love story.

But will anyone love me?

Why would anybody stick with me if my own parents didn't?

Will anyone ever care enough to stay with me?

If no one does, will I ever find out why I was born, find my home? Find my own voice?

The answer hangs in midair, and I'm stunned. The answer looks back at me as if I know what to do with it.

All I can think to say is, "If I write a love story, I want it to be the best love story ever written." A love story that doesn't just end with "and they lived happily ever after," as if life stopped, trapped in those words.

I want a story of a love that reaches into the middle of pain, suffering, and struggle, that pulls the girl out, leading her to a beautiful homeland, the land her heart relentlessly ached for from the beginning. I want her to travel there on the arm of her lover. I want it to be a never-ending pilgrimage of belonging.

What is this? A breadcrumb, and I take and eat. For the first time, I feel full. How can one breadcrumb fill me so much? It's a mystery. I scribble a mental note: If I eat breadcrumbs, I can move from scared to sacred.

I can feel it, the start of a journey. I have a long way to go. But the breadcrumbs are beckoning me along a path, and I know I must follow. So I try.

I want to write the best love story ever written with you. My story doesn't need words; it is written in the stars for everyone to see. Soon, my brave one, we will look at those stars together. True north will lead you home. All my words are livable. My words are for hearts. For the interior places. You feel the longings, desires, and dreams. At first, words are everywhere, and you eat them, taking you where you don't want to go. Listen, little one, when you can't see me, follow my breadcrumbs. Follow them to others who eat my words and hear my voice. Follow those whose first love is me.

You may not know it yet, but I am writing a lifeline of words that you can hang on to for dear life. This lifeline will pull you up, fill your longing, and carry you to safety.

There is a promised land on the other side of the wilderness, my love.

My words are homing devices leading you back home. Back to me.

Listen for my words; they are finding you.

My words
are homing
d e v i c e s
l e a d i n g
you back
home.
Back to me.
—Papa

chapter

eight

Welcome Mat

No one has told me why I am being shipped from my mom's house to live with my dad and stepmom. Norman and Mom divorced. My sister and I are sent to our dad's. My little brother stays with my mom.

I don't know my dad or my stepmom. I've only visited a handful of times. Grandma told me I cried because I didn't know him so I didn't have to go anymore. Until today. I am unhinged and hungry for a rhythm of home. I knock on the door after being dropped off at my dad and stepmom's house.

The house has all the things that make me think it is home: two parents, a dining room table with chairs, bunk beds with matching eyelet-trimmed floral comforters. It appears perfect. Except there is no welcome mat.

Dad opens the door.

"Come in, sugar," he says, giving me a hug and kissing my head. The words are something a dad would say, but his voice sounds broken down and falling apart and somehow abandoned. Behind my dad a wind howls through the house, groaning, wanting out. Nothing here is familiar. I want to run but I'm trapped.

I'm nine and I can't turn off; this primitive cry inside begs me to open my mouth to the heavens and let it out. I want to go home, but even my mom's house—the only home I can remember wanting—doesn't want me. I buck up, thinking maybe this will be the place where I find help. Probably not.

My stepmom doesn't seem to like me much. She says as much with her eyes and cutting words. She's always searching for something to make herself and Dad look good enough. I don't like her games. I don't know the rules, except that appearance is everything. Maybe to my stepmom I am a fragmented, hard to love little girl who thinks too much and feels too deep and doesn't know how to hide it.

I get asthma living with Dad and my stepmom, and this also bothers my stepmom. A sickly kid interrupts gymnastic class, Girl Scouts, and fitting in. Every night, like punishment, she tells me to sit against the wall and get out my breathing treatment. I plug it in and put the vials of medicine in and flip the switch. I try to stop the sickness from coming so I can play and earn her love, but I can't. I don't like watching everyone else from the wall; they seem to love my sister so well.

It's a few nights after moving in, and the doorbell rings. I open the door and look up at an overgrown man with unruly hair and round glasses. "This is the pastor of the church," Dad tells me, and I size him up. He seems kind. He smiles at me and I smile back. I join them at the dinner table and eat my spaghetti with no sauce, as usual. I say my pleases and thank-yous at the dinner table, and after eating, ask to be excused. Dad, my stepmom, and the pastor gather at the front door at the end of the night. I follow them.

How can I ask for help? How can I ask him to protect me, to get me out of here? Can I ask him for the way home? Ask him what my name is? The pastor will help, I'm sure of it. It's now or never. My heart throbs in my chest, and before I can think another thought, I step into the middle of them and raise my dad's shirt, exposing the acne on his back.

"See," I say, "my dad has zits on his back."

Standing in front of the pastor, shame kidnaps me. I don't want to be kidnapped by shame; I want to be kidnapped by someone who will take me where there are not fake homes, fake smiles, and fake pastors. Here it comes again, the deluge of voices.

I don't have anyone but myself.

Who is taking care of me?

I am alone in the middle of a nightmare.

I am an embarrassment.

I don't know how to fit in with people. In fact, I don't know anything.

I'm a stupid little girl.

I shouldn't be lost and want to go home.

I feel the pastor's uneasiness in his fake smile, hear his thoughts in his hand running nervously over his Bible. He doesn't say anything, but still, I hear him.

Good luck with that, kid. I've got enough pain of my own and can't take time to touch yours.

I turn and run up the spiral staircase to my room and throw myself on the bottom bunk, looking for a place to hide because I know what's coming. I open my heart like a suitcase, shoving the voices inside, but my heart is so jammed full. Can I sit on top of my heart? Will that keep those voices in?

I hear the pastor leave and the door shut. My stepmom is angry. I hear her muffled voice talking to my dad. There are thoughts behind those words, though, and I can hear those thoughts climbing the staircase. They tuck themselves in bed with me. They whisper.

What is wrong with you?

Are you broken and there is no fix?

You've done it now.

There is no way back home.

You're stupid and an embarrassment.

I sob all night and into the morning.

The sun rises and I pay the price for telling the truth to the pastor. The whipping with the flyswatter my stepmom gives me when Dad is gone bites the back of my thighs, but the sting somehow begins to feel good. Yes, I deserve to be punished for being stupid, for not pretending, for telling the truth, for outing my dad's secrets.

My stepmom tells me not to tell Dad, but cold water can't wash the evidence away. After work, Dad pretends not to notice. Maybe daddies pretend instead of protect.

Do you even like me, Daddy?

Aren't I your little girl?

I feel like the fly swatter has smashed my heart again.

You do not deserve this, sweet one. I am crushed every time you are. Little one, I am with you, helping you. See? Hear? Not yet, but you will. I see. I hear. I never avert my eyes or turn my head when children are hurt. I'm acting on your behalf since you cannot.

I am hiding you in my shadow, and it will be your safe place. I am your safe person. You won't always be watching life from against a wall; you will be living life taking me at my word. You don't have to get yourself together, little one. Let me come get you, pick you up just as you are. But I won't leave you that way. I am awakening a hunger inside you. Soon, you will let me feed you. Eat my words.

Remember, you are always at home here, always welcome.

nine

Play Pretend

I live in a house, but it is not a home. There is no trust here. Or with my mom. I become my home. Inside myself, I can control what I can't on the outside. I dig tunnels inside myself where it's dark. I like the dark because I can hide. I can hide what's wrong with me. I sometimes escape my life by living in those burrows with my buried feelings and memories.

Maybe Dad sits on the sidelines because his own voice was quieted and now he burrows into his own skin. When it is just my dad, my sister, and me, we go to the store, and he buys us ice-cold Cokes in glass bottles, letting us pull our own out of the machine. I love pulling the bottle out and waiting for the glass to clink as the next bottle slides into place. He tells funny jokes, and we laugh till our sides hurt. One time my stepmom told him to spank us. When he bent us over his knee, he smiled and told us to cry out like it really hurt. We giggled and did what he said. I like Dad when my stepmom isn't around.

When my stepmom is around, things are different. I'm different than everyone else. I'm not liked as much as my sister, who's good at playing along. I fight back too much. Like the time my stepmom let my sister get bangs, but she told me no. Later in the week I took the scissors to my hair in the school bathroom. She was mortified that I would do such a thing and sent me to my room until she could talk to my dad. I picked up the phone in our bedroom, overhearing her talking to her sister, Aunt Jackie. She told her I looked ugly with bangs. I covered the receiver and put it back in the cradle as quietly as I could. And cried.

Is looking a certain way the key for me to be seen? For someone to hear me? Is there something on the outside of me that is in the way? I am different. I don't know how to hide it. Does anyone understand?

I can't stop my insides from trembling when I catch a glimpse of her looking at me as if I'm to conceal something. She hands me a coffee cup full of pills. I ask her what they are. She tells me they are vitamins. That I am sickly. She says they are alfalfa tablets. Six of them. And some others.

"Take them," she says.

But it's so much to swallow.

She is bigger than me, not just in size but like something invisible in her wants to crush something in me down to size.

I'm terrified of her. I can feel the darkness in her, the lies, the meanness. Sometimes I think she knows that I know who she really is. She is the playground bully. If I do everything her way, if I keep my head down and my feelings to myself, I'll be okay, but not safe.

What's more, I see her sides—the side she shows at home and the side she shows when we aren't. She bakes cookies for the neighbors, and we pretend pretty when we go out. We pull back our hair into pigtails, tie them up with bows. We never walk out just like we are. We hide behind our do-goods and look-goods.

None of this is real though. Am I? Am I a doll? Why do I feel so pretend?

I attend a Christian school where everyone seems to appreciate do-goods and look-goods too. It is very strict. Today is report card day, my least favorite day of school. I am not doing well in school. I know it isn't because I'm not smart; the chaos makes it impossible to think. My heart sinks as I take the yellow envelope from Miss Z because I know what it says. It screams, "You're a failure. You're in trouble. And there is no one on your side to help."

I step off the van and run to my room, shutting the door behind me, and begin rummaging through my book bag to retrieve the report card. I think I can change the Fs to Es by adding a line. Will my stepmom be able to tell? I grab a pen from my bag and in one stroke I change the shape of my life.

She calls from the dining room like a dinner bell. "Come to the table. It's time for dinner," she says, and held in fear, my skin pulls up extra tight as I walk downstairs. We pass the green beans, answer questions about our day, listen to our list of to-dos after dinner: take baths, brush teeth, and feed the dog. She's already laid out our clothes.

It's my favorite time of the day—after our bath. I begin to feel sorry about the way I feel about my stepmom. Maybe she's not so bad. Every night after our bath, my stepmom blow-dries our hair. The rhythmic brushing and the warmth of the hair dryer lull me close to feeling held. Then she curls our hair up in pink sponge rollers. Even though they hurt to sleep on, somehow it makes me feel loved. I feel loved when she brushes, blow-dries, and fixes my hair.

Then she asks, "Did you girls get report cards today?"

My sister nods. "Yes," she says, smiling. She wants to go first. We are excused to go get them. I get up off the floor and walk up to my room to get my report card. Somebody isn't going to be okay. It's them or me. Dread walks with me back downstairs. Will they know I changed the letters? How far do I have to go for someone to pay attention? Realize that I'm not okay?

Is anyone noticing that my heartbeats aren't connecting in rhythm? Maybe it's because my heart is broken.

Dad doesn't catch me, but my stepmom does, and she lets me know what I did is wrong. Her eyes bore holes in my heart, then her words, like ink, tattoo themselves on the skin of my heart. Like she knew exactly how to get under my skin.

"You want so badly to go back home to live with your mom? Well now you get what you want!" she screams. "I'm done!" she screams again. She keeps hollering, telling me I've disrupted their lives enough, that I came with nothing, I'll leave with nothing, and that I can take my sister with me.

In disgust she sends me to my room, tells me that making my sister leave is part of the punishment. My sister is happy here, she says. Everything is my fault.

In the middle of the night I pick up the phone and call Grandma, crying for her to come get me. I even threaten to run away. I say I will go to the 7-Eleven up the street and call her from the pay phone. She tells me she can't, tells me to lie in bed and talk to God. She'll try and help me tomorrow.

"Don't cry, baby doll," she says before she hangs up the phone.

I get back into bed, bury my face in my pillow, and ask God to please help me. Come and get me. Please let me go back and live with Mom. Please.

I go back to Mom's house the way I came—with a trash bag of belongings. My stepmom keeps most everything—our toys, our school clothes, our bedding. All of it. Even my puppet from Granny that she brought back from Germany, and our record player, and the Alvin and the Chipmunks records. How come it hurts so much that she is keeping all my things, even though I'm not coming back? Why don't nice things make a place feel like a home?

I am your shelter-of-story. I get down on my hands and knees in the middle of your unknown and wash you, brush your hair, and hold your hand. Let me take all the hurt-words and give you soul-medicine.

Little one, look me in the eyes. Look at me. I delight to give you treasures. Treasures with no strings. I am giving you an inheritance. Treasure by treasure. My treasures can be found in darkness. Don't be afraid of the darkness, little one. Look for my breadcrumbs in it. My words, they are your searchlight. My words are looking for you, finding you. My hands are always working to help you, hold you, and heal you. My hands hold home inside you because I'm your home. Little one, once we've written your story, you will *never* come back home the way you came.

Little one, your heart holds your something-more. I tucked it inside like a homing device, to turn you around and lead you back to my heart. Reach out and take your something-more when the time comes. I won't take it back. It is forever yours.

Needing Medicine

'm thirteen. Instead of walking to the trailer park, reading a book on the back porch, or hanging at my friend's house eating Ramen noodles, I'm reading Mom and my stepdad's heartbeats more than their mouths. The TV is blaring but I'm not listening. I feel the words in my body before I hear them in my head. My heart begins racing and my stomach feels nauseous.

Here we go again.

Stepdad Larry says, "Who ate the cereal?" I feel the temperature in the house go from cold to hot in the asking of the question. Mom doesn't work right now because she is nursing my baby sister. The food budget is tight, and stepkids are an added expense when there is no child support. The argument escalates, Mom yelling at us to get our stuff, get in the car, we are going to Grandma's.

We come back the next day, like we always do, to make ups that make me sick. I go to my bedroom so I don't have to watch them pretend again, when all I want to do is pull the fire alarm and have the firefighters come rescue me. I wish somebody would tell the truth. I wish Mom would say, "We can't help you because we are sick, our marriage is sick. We can't even help ourselves."

I want to say we need a doctor. We need medicine. But I don't. Instead, I take my feelings to my room so I don't have to watch them pretend. So I don't have to pretend.

Pain drives my heart, and it follows no map, has no direction in mind. I crave constant motion or commotion, and daydreams hijack my heart, pushing it into fantasy and fairy tale. A voice says, "This is the way, walk in it," but chaos pushes me to my bedroom window.

I kneel on the carpet, play "Jack & Diane" on the cassette player, and open the window so the boy next door can hear the music. His family moved next door last week, and his trailer window sits only twenty feet from mine.

The music plays, and I lean against the window screen, daydreaming, watching the high school boy next door and his brothers cut out weeds with butter knives. It is early spring, and the breeze coming in my window smells like fresh cut grass. The boy I'm watching must be in high school because he can drive. In my daydreams, he is in his Pontiac LeMans, windows down, this song blaring. I am in the passenger seat, singing along with him. We are two American kids growing up in the heartland.

Could this boy be the one? One-two-three, will he catch me? I am thirteen and no one has caught me except a doctor in the delivery room.

Before I have time to sing "Diane's sittin' on Jacky's lap," the window screen pops out. I scream and fall through, and now I'm dangling by my belt loops, hanging half out of the window. Butter knives go flying as the high school boy comes running.

Little one, I am your map, your compass, your true north. My words are signposts leading you home. I am your shelter-of-story.

—Papa

He puts one hand on my waist and one on my shoulder to help pull me up, and it feels like his hands form an attachment to the aching inside me, the ache asking the back and forth to please stop. I'm wanting someone to hear the sounds I hear, to help me do something about them. Maybe his hands can help all this chaos, help steady me.

Maybe he is the help I want.

I want to grab hold of this boy with both hands and beg him to save me. He is different, gentle, and he doesn't try to touch my butt like my friend's creepy brother. Instead, he helps me up. He feels warm and soft, and all I want is for him to hold all of me together forever.

His smile matches his eyes, giving me permission to be at ease. I don't know why I feel the way I do when I look at him. I just hope he is my "once upon a time" like Jack was for Diane.

After dinner, I pour my thoughts into a notebook and begin to write, like I used to at Grandma's, back when I made a hideaway under the kitchen table and chairs and scribbled on notepads.

I sit here in bed listening to "Endless Love," writing about my day with scented markers in my notebook covered with stickers and doodles, looking out my bedroom window, remembering how it felt when he caught me. Like I came out of the shadows a bit when our eyes saw each other. I can't stop wondering if he can help me, if he can help me put words on the scattered emptiness inside me. I can see his house from my bed. I wonder if he's thinking about me too.

I write out all of my madness and sadness about my mom and stepdad moving to the trailer park from our house in Blue Springs. I had a friend next door, Dana; I was getting ready to start junior high school; and her brother Richard liked me. We had even formed a band in the basement of my house. Now everything has been ripped away, again. I thought living with Mom would make the ache go away, but it hasn't. As I write, I wonder if it made it worse.

I write how happy I am after falling into this boy's arms. It gave me hope today. Hope that he can take my mind off what is happening in my insides, in our house. The happy feels like the words in this song, so I push rewind, playing it over and over.

Maybe this is why we moved to the trailer park. So the boy next door and I could meet so we can give each other everything. Maybe I can give him all my love, and he can help carry my ache inside. Maybe if we are together the ache will go away. Maybe his love will be the medicine I need.

I sense Papa's smile as I squeeze my notebook tight to my chest, smiling at the new page I got to write tonight. My first love. I smile again before turning out the lights, lyrics pulling me into dreams. Dreams about what it would look like for him to ask me to be his girlfriend. I wonder if I will see him tomorrow. If he will be outside.

Little one, I am your map, your compass, your true north. My words are signposts leading you home. I am your shelter-of-story.

I always bend low where you are, answering your feelings of not enough with the truth of my more than enough. I am always talking to the tiny warrior in you. Until one day when you become my mighty, beloved warrior daughter. I am training you for battle. Forging you into an arrow. I will use your life to aim you in the right direction. I will use every battle for your good and my glory. Am I not the God of angel armies?

My beautiful girl, I am hovering over your story. I am book-ending you, little one. I am the beginning, the end, and the content in between. Little one, as you take and eat my words, each of our story's chapters marry each other like pearls strung on a delicate string—one day to be a keepsake to treasure in your heart.

I have living words to give you to hold on to. Little one, hold on to my words with both hands. Let my words pull you all the way out of the shadows, little one. You are made to walk in my glory.

chapter

eleven

Grown-Ups

I haven't gone to church in four years—since the year I lived with Dad and my stepmom.

I go with Ronnie (the boy next door), his mom, and his brothers. His dad stays home. His mom sings in the choir.

Every week they pull up in front of my house and take me to church. It's about four miles. We drive down an outer road, past the Bates City Mini Mart, then Bates City BBQ, cross the railroad tracks, come to a three-way stop, and we're there. The youth group is planning a canoe trip this summer. Ronnie and I ask if we can go. Our parents say yes.

It's the first time I'm allowed to go with him alone. I'm restless and agitated, wondering if there is something more out there. Something beyond this trailer park filled with dilapidated single-wides full of hurt people, lost people, angry people, and confused people. I feel the pain of their poverty. I'm sure there are some happy people too. I am distracted. Questions unravel me. I want to grow up and get out, and it can't happen fast enough.

We sit in the cab of his dad's Chevy Silverado pickup, "Tainted Love" playing on the radio as we pull into the driveway. It's past ten, the front porch light on my trailer telling me it is time to go inside. I don't want to say goodbye after a long weekend away. We spent the days canoeing and swimming and the nights roasting marshmallows around the campfire and kissing behind trees.

We came back drunk on pretending to be grown-up and parentless. Our clothes smell like lake water. Our kisses feel like the warmth of the sun radiating off the water. The windows are down; cicadas hum; I feel summer's intoxication. I kiss him again.

"I don't want to go home," I whisper. Ronnie says he feels the same.

"Do you ever wonder what it would be like to be married?" I ask.

"Ah . . . kind of," he says.

I do, I say to myself. I wonder myself out of reality into imagining what it would be like to have a baby of my own. Would it be a boy or girl? What would it look like? Would it have my blue eyes or his brown? Taking care of my baby sister makes me yearn to have someone of my own to love and care for.

"I'm tired of being told what to do," I tell him.

I am tired of figuring out what is real and what isn't. I want to know for myself.

This something-more out there somewhere pulls me to fill the void of shapelessness of my life. Maybe I want Ronnie to hear me, see me behind the glass, break the walls around my life, and help me escape. Maybe I just want him to make me free.

"I think we could make it together," I tell him. "We can escape our lives and make something new. Something good."

This weekend is what it would feel like. He smiles at me like I hung the moon, and we kiss some more. My thoughts interrupt mid-kissing, they are running so fast.

"I can get a job after school," I blurt out. "You graduate next year and can work full time at the shoe store." I have it all figured out.

He pulls me close, missing me already.

"Let's talk to our parents," I say.

"Tiff!" he laughs, but the kind of laugh that shows he doesn't know if I'm kidding or not.

I'm not kidding, I say in my head. I'm dead serious.

Ronnie's family has something I want. They know stability: a dad who is a high-class truck driver and makes good money, even if he plays around with cigarettes and women behind his wife's back; a mom who is supportive and has a steady job working for an insurance company. She is a sun pulling everyone into her orbit. Dinner is like a clock, running on her time. She teaches me that butter knives aren't only for cutting out weeds, they are also for cutting the air when it is stretched like a tightrope across a dinner table.

All my life I have never known what was coming next. I've never known a family dinner table. A pool table sits where our dining table should, and we eat around the TV. My stepdad is a truck driver, but not a high-class one. There are three kids, no child support, and my mom stays home with my baby sister, sewing little girl dresses for side money. Food stamps are our currency. Even though we live in a trailer, it's a new one and the nicest in the park. We've finally found some sort of stability, and though I should want to stick around, I know I won't. I don't want to.

Our families are so different. His parents view life as a sort of boot camp meant to be worked for and run on a tight schedule. To my mom and stepdad, life is a game. Like I'm on my own. Play at my own risk. To me, everything feels like life or death, and it matters how I live life. To me, there is this something-more inside me. It calls to me to love it with everything in me. Ronnie and I talk about being on our own during our drives to church, in his bedroom while our parents play cards, and on the way home from school. Ronnie and I can't live the lives we've been dealt, so we decide to tell our parents we want to get married.

On the next game night, our parents are playing poker around our pool table, and we tell them. They lay down their cards and ask if we are serious. We are. As they protest, something rises up in me at the injustice of all the past years, and I lay all my cards on the table.

Ronnie can't believe the things I am saying: it doesn't matter I am underage, that he is just a shoe salesman, that we can't support ourselves, or that I am still in school. I fight for us in that living room, even threatening to run away. I'm hungry to follow this something out there that tells me there is a way of escape, and I will find it at any cost.

By the end of the night, both sets of parents agree to our marriage, my mom promising to sign the documents needed for a minor marriage if we will wait a year. Our pastor, Brother Don, agrees to marry us if we go through premarital counseling.

Over the next year, while I wait to turn sixteen, our parents play cards together on weekends. We listen to music and go as far as we can without having sex. I don't tell him the truth—that I'm embarrassed for him to see me naked. I don't know why, other than something inside me feels dirty. I didn't know it was there until we were going too far kissing, and he tried to go farther but I couldn't. It's invisible but it's real. I tell him I want to wait until we're married. So we do.

Brother Don tells us in premarital counseling that we have God's blessing. I don't want to do anything wrong to upset God and not be blessed. We pass premarital counseling better than his grown-up couples, Brother Don says. Nobody has ever been proud of me like him. Bates City Baptist church is for us; we are their trophy. Our youth leaders use us as examples of how young love can work, how to be good kids. This place begins to feel like a home.

I check off the days like a Christmas countdown calendar. In one year I will be Ronnie's wife. At fifteen, I am filled with visions that whet my appetite of how it will look when I walk down the aisle, have babies, and live in a home that doesn't move.

There is no proposal, no pursuing, and no bended knee, but I want out more than I care what happens to me.

I can see my happily-ever-after coming true, my words pulled from my notebooks and pieced together on us like paper dolls, not a real-life boy and girl.

Little one, stop and listen to my voice. Stop cutting out pieces of your heart and giving them away, pieces that will cost you more than you will be able to give. I want to be your first love.

The best love story ever written, my love, is ours. Together. Let me write *with* you. Take my words for you. Do what they say. Let me lift your heart and turn it to me. I will take time with you. I won't just tell you, I will show you how. I will help.

I listen to everything you have to say. Your cry never wearies me. I will not leave you fatherless, motherless, or friendless. I want to give you safe people. Even now, I am creating a safety net of people for you. I am shaping your heart right side up, restoring it. I am bigger than your human eyes can see. I am setting you up to sit you down in a fixed place. I put a traveler's heart in you, but it isn't to be homeless. I am your fixed place. I am your perfect home. I know you don't know what having a home—one that doesn't move—looks like, feels like. Moving is familiar. Staying is not. Let me show you.

chapter
twelve

Honeymoon

I am standing on a pedestal in front of a mirror. For sixteen years I've tried to figure out what is wrong with me, tried to stop feeling so much, and instead, hid so everyone else would be okay. Today I'm camouflaged as a bride-to-be, as if I'm sitting on the top shelf of some trophy case. If I'm sweet and don't talk, keep my feelings, thoughts, and perceptions to myself, then everyone will be okay.

My mom, sisters, two friends, and I sit in a wedding dress shop located in a strip mall six miles from our trailer park. I can't believe I was thirteen years old when I fell out of my bedroom window into the arms of the boy next door, and now, three years and an ambiguous yes in the dark cab of a Chevy pickup truck later, here I am.

I put imaginary headphones on to muffle the noise of the room, so I can hear what's happening below the surface, below the skin of all these people. I watch lips move, heads nod; there is conversation. I feel their impressions, the way a face looks away and down, eyebrows arch in question and lips purse. I'm not so sure about this, their expressions say. I know their questions aren't really directed at me. They're searching for their own something-more, something that will give them love, maybe definition. They are locked up, and they push back their pain. Sometimes I wish I didn't have this gift or curse, whatever it is, but I can't seem to quit the compulsion to quiet the noise so I can hear underneath.

I hear beneath my own surface too. I'm ashamed of myself all the way past my naked skin. I can't put my finger on it. Why am I ashamed? I don't know why I don't like seeing myself in mirrors or people looking at me. Maybe because others can see what's missing, what's wrong, what I can't seem to find and fix. I want to dump my thoughts and impressions out; I want someone who will make sense of them with me. I want to be seen, heard, known, and loved. Maybe even held. Let me be seen naked by the boy next door, but even then, there's something I can't fully explain to him. And even if I could express it, he couldn't handle it, the bareness of it.

I don't think any human can.

Maybe that is why people wear masks, to hide their shame so they aren't called on the carpet. I wonder about things like this all the time. To connect, I need to be known, and not for look-goods and do-goods. I want to be known for me, the real me. Do I know what or whom that is? Deep down I wonder if I could let all my shame out, let someone see every piece of ugly in me, tell the truth, the entire truth about myself. It might make me feel like I am dying, but deep down I know that's when I would really begin to live.

The closest I come to feeling known is at church. In church, when Brother Don opens the Bible and reads the words inside, my blood runs gospel, and my heart beats ancient. My heart opens, and words wash my heart. I can't explain it, but I write about it in my journals at night.

It happens at home, in the car, and today while I'm doing laundry for the last time in Mom's house. I sense God everywhere. I know God isn't contained in a building; he's a real Being. I smile because my life is working out the way I dreamed it would. Hearing God feels like standing in Grandma's backyard, under the tree, where the tall grass grows. I used to tilt my head heavenward, put my arms straight out on either side, close my eyes, and turn around and around and around, the tall grass tickling my hands.

I still can't believe I will have my own home. I won't have to go hide when it is God and me. I seem to make people uncomfortable when I talk about him. My mom, dad, stepmom, and Ronnie don't see him the way I do, as a real Person. Maybe to them God is a fantasy, a crutch that weak people need or maybe a make-believe story. But to me, he is my searchlight. He helps me see in dark places. Around me. In me.

Maybe I make them uncomfortable when I bring him home from church with me. Maybe they believe he is supposed to stay in the church and only on Sunday, when someone dies, or when there is an emergency.

On the pedestal, looking into the mirror, I make a decision. I lift my heart like a rug and sweep God under, refocus. Right now, all I have are eyes for this boy, my almost husband. The words of all those novels, my grandfather's notebooks, my own notebooks—all those words—lure me to lose myself in his protection. Even if he doesn't know the real me, can't he shield me from all the people who don't seem to understand me?

The day of the wedding, the last pins go in my dress, in my hair. It is time to walk another aisle. No ornate stone church or expansive choir alcove. Only a simple, white country church with a steeple and a pastor I adore. I walk this aisle on the arm of my eleven-year-old brother. On one side of the aisle, I hear them—*you're going to fail*—and on the other side I hear the other voices—*you're too young.*

I have a sweet-sixteen wedding, all pink, mauve, and burgundy. My little sister is the flower girl. My dad's family didn't come, but I am surrounded by my grandma, mom, and church family. My two friends and my sister stand with me.

At the altar, Ronnie waits for me. We exchange vows. We kiss. Pastor tells us we are now one. *One, what does that mean? Does it mean I'm not me anymore? Am I not one all by myself?*

We get into the back seat of our new Ford Escort, covered in shaving cream, crepe paper streamers, and pop cans, and the questions fade as my smile stretches all the way down to my heart. It's so big it hurts. I look at my husband and can't believe I'm married. I know this is the beginning of my life. My dreams are finally coming true. The best love story ever written, coming true.

We can't afford a honeymoon, so Grandma offers her house. She stays with my mom and leaves the refrigerator stocked. There are flowers in a vase and a card telling me I am her baby doll. Inside the card are two tickets to the movie theater. We consummate the marriage in the room where I stayed when I came home from the hospital. It's the room I found my grandpa and his unfinished notepads in. We become one in a double bed, and it is supposed to be the happiest day of my life, but I begin to cry. I cry for my little sister. I cry that I am like my mother. I cry for missing home and cry for Grandma's vase of flowers. I cry for the sex we waited for, sex that isn't at all like I dreamed it would be. I cry for feeling dirty, for wanting to run and wash myself. In the making of love, disappointment creeps in quietly, not in my husband but in myself. I didn't get it right again? What is wrong with me? How? But I love Ronnie. He is all I have, and I give everything to him, almost. I hide away that piece, that something-more that throbs in my heart, the notepads that fell at my feet outside Grandpa's closet when I was nine. I roll over, looking at that closet tonight.

You see yourself as a peculiar thing that is embarrassing, hideous, and dirty, too much and yet not enough. Little one, you are not a secret to hide.

Shame holds you hostage. Shame is the real abuser. She will not save you when you self-destruct.

But truth has a voice here too. I am telling you that you are not crazy. I've been here all along, countering every move of the enemy in your life.

I make hearts uncomfortable. I do. My light shines on the places in hearts that hurt. That need gospel-medicine. People hide from my searchlight. Hide what they don't want seen. Touched. Don't let shame tell you who you are. It isn't you. Secrets are making you sick. Secrets create shame. I will help lead you to people who are safe. I will find you in my story, my words picking you up, placing you in your scene. Chapter and verse. Not a moment too late.

When I see you, I don't see what's wrong. I see what isn't there yet. I see all the places we get to work and play together. I see where we are going to grow closer. Places where we will fall in love. I see your deepness. I put it there. I am calling you deeper. I am teaching you deep things in deep places. Let me hold you, love you, and wash your heart with my words. Let me do for you what you can't do for yourself.

My love, come to me as *I am*. I am always leaning down, ready to lift you up.

chapter
thirteen

Last Supper

Grandma cosigns the loan, and we buy a run-down two-bedroom single-wide trailer, and we set up house with our own bedroom furniture and hand-me-downs. We move down the street from my mom and stepdad the summer before my junior year in high school, and I find a waitress job at a truck stop three miles down the road. Ronnie works as a shoe sales associate at Payless ShoeSource.

Ronnie didn't say no to a baby when I asked. I think he wants to have a happily-ever-after too. I spend the days obsessed with getting pregnant and the nights "trying," after which our conversation drifts to how we both want a girl. It would be the first girl on his side of the family in a long time, and how cool it will be that our baby would be the first grandbaby on both sides. The months of waiting for a yes are filled with library hauls of pregnancy books, setting up a nursery with my little sister's hand-me-downs, and perusing secondhand stores for baby clothes.

We try for eight months, and I can't get pregnant. My inability to stop the ache to have a baby chews at the hem of my heart, leaving me distracted and annoyed. I stalk the calendar, wondering whether my period will be late or not. I can't focus on anything but a baby.

The morning the yes comes in the form of a pink plus sign, I reach up, taking from God's hand, like a beggar takes a handout in a soup kitchen line. I cry broken hallelujahs on my knees on the bathroom floor between the toilet and the tub. I stay here for a long time with God, not believing what he has done for me. I struggle to receive the gift, that God gave me an answer, a yes, a dream even though I can't find the time to go to church.

I tell Ronnie later in the morning that I'm pregnant, but I don't share the moment that God, this little baby, and I had together on the bathroom floor. This is my memory, and I'll live in it for as long as I can because I am learning that my dreams don't feel like they did in the notebooks.

My days are soon filled with battling all-day morning sickness. At the dishwashing station at the truck stop, the food scraped off the plates and thrown into a disposal send me running to the employee bathroom that reeks of old grease and bleach and urine. I watch the contents of my stomach spiral down the rust-crusted toilet, and all I want is to die.

I leave my job with that smell pressed into my uniform and pores. Truck drivers' starving eyes follow my curves, up one side and down the other like I could be their last meal. Do they know all I have to give them are scraps? School takes bites out of me when I walk the halls in handmade maternity clothes. Raging hormones cause my acne to flare up, and after I cut all my hair off like Olivia Newton-John, I suddenly feel like a boy. I am the only pregnant girl in school, and I am like a creature from another planet. Everyone, teachers included, think I'm a problem to be fixed. I'm permanently pockmarked by high school gossip; I see my classmates hiding whispers. I wear paranoia like a sweater turned inside out.

I can barely keep up with school all day and then working an eight-hour shift at the truck stop. I look forward to the bus ride home from school so I can hide behind sleep. I look forward to being back in our trailer where I can take off the paranoia and cry. I look forward to the day when I feel like a real adult.

Going to school pregnant, keeping my grades up, and waiting tables to make ends meet begins to stir the pot of panic lying dormant. Ronnie comes home after a long day at work and finds me on the couch, stripped from my waitress dress, which barely fits anymore. I am in a dress that looks like my grandma's muumuu, a big swath of fabric. I'm crying because I lost my body to stretch marks and my hair to a hormonal knee-jerk decision. I'm crying because we have no food, no money, and no way out. I'm crying because this all feels like it did growing up, and I know how that goes.

He looks at his hands and he puts them in mine and gives me everything he has in this moment. He asks me to stop crying, says he will cook something to eat. He turns the last bits in our cabinet into a last supper. Hamburger, a can of beans, tomato juice, a pinch of seasoning. The smell wafting from the kitchen bypasses my stomach and goes straight to my heart. Maybe it wasn't so much my body that was hungry after all; maybe it is my hungry heart tasting what feels like home for the first time in a long time.

This is what home feels like: a meal prepared with hands, the ingredients "everything" someone has. I want to taste this home again. The ancientness of it feeds something deep down, unexplored. I know I will want that feeling again and again and again. What is that feeling? Is it belonging?

I look into the quiet while we eat soup around the TV like we did at my mom and stepdad's. After he finishes, he passes out on the couch, just like that. No conversation. No planning. Nothing. I check his pulse with my eyes. Is he breathing? How come I want to throw soup at him, scalding him awake—or maybe alive? An inexplicable feeling sits in the middle of the room with us. I can't put my finger on it though. I am scared and angry at him for not doing something, anything, to let me know it will be okay, that we're okay.

Am I the only one seeing this? I want to ask. *I don't know what to do!* I blubber inside like a baby. *I'm scared, and I need you to help me do something. Help me fix this. Us. Me. Be my partner, support me, lead me, don't tap out. I need more than food. I need words from you. Talk to me about what we can do.*

I want to scream it. But I don't. Instead, while he sleeps, I turn words I want to say to him, words I say to me, on myself. Scarcity holds my heart down while I let my heart have it good. And I don't stop until I run out of energy and words.

After Christmas break the school staff tires of me disrupting the halls between classes and maybe feels a bit sorry for me too. Not knowing what to do with me, they offer me homebound placement. I can do my work at home and come in once a week and go over my work with a teacher. I do my best, but after a month, I quit.

Halfway through my senior year, I give up my education for a baby. Something had to go. That something was me.

I am present in the tiniest fibers of your reality. I am not wishful thinking, a storybook knight in shining armor, or an enabler. I am as real as the nose on your face. Let me lead you, be your lifelong partner. You know what to do, little one. Trust me. A husband can help, but he isn't me.

You will come out on the other side. Reach for what could be. Reach for me. I'm reaching for you.

I am in the innermost part of your heart. It's where my home is. Everywhere you go, I go.

In every hard circumstance and decision, when everything feels like it did growing up, I'm in it with you. You feel trapped, but I am bent low, reaching for you. Take my hand. I will help you navigate your way out of the pain, the feeling of being trapped in your skin. You clutch yourself, your husband, your grandma, your baby—anything and everything but me. Driven to keep everything and everyone together. In all of that energy, you can't keep yourself together.

When you finally understand your hunger for me, for the something-more, everything will turn. Your appetite is taking you the wrong way for now, toward emptiness. But do not fear, little one. You're not lost. I know where you are. I restore what was lost. Remember, I am your finding place. Trust the instinct of the tiny bird inside you. I am always dropping breadcrumbs. Breadcrumbs that will lead you back home. When you finally take and eat my Word, you'll be full.

I am present in the tiniest fibers of your reality. I am not wishful thinking,

a storybook knight in shining armor,

or an enabler. I am as real as

the nose on your face.

—Papa

fourteen

Birth

A re you ready to have a baby today?" the nurse asks. The nurse comments on how young I am. I smile at her. Smiling covers my big feelings. It's my default mechanism. Smiles can cover a multitude of uncertainties.

Lying back in bed, I answer the nurse's questions. I tell her I don't know how to have a baby. I tell her I don't know what a good mom looks like. But I want to be one. I want to make it count. I know it matters. I tell her more than anything I want to be a mom. I didn't try to find it, the want to have a baby. Somehow it's always been there. Inside me.

I feel like a dream is coming true today. Like a cake, candles, and a party. Today Ronnie and I are going to have a baby.

The hospital stirs, a vortex of life and death. I take a deep breath, shoot the tiny cup of pain meds quickly so I don't have to taste them going down. I come out of the bathroom, scan the small room—a box unadorned except for two chairs, a rocker, and a bed. I'm not meant to be comfortable here.

I don't know if I'm ready to have the baby; maybe I won't be able to handle the pain.

I vacillate between pain and fear, worrying if I will know how to push correctly. I shudder at the thought of a room full of people watching me with legs wide open, pushing out my new baby. It is more than I am ready for. As my labor progresses, though, I stop caring about the embarrassment and pain. I rise up, charge forward.

I go deep, breathing my way through contraction after contraction. The pain, each contraction, like a mountain I climb. Each peak followed by a quick descent, directing me to the next mountain. And I climb the next one.

I am wide awake in this pain. Tapping out for drugs isn't an option anymore. Pain interrogates me ruthlessly, and I can't escape into dreams. Pain holds my face in vise-grips, and I look at it head-on. Pain is an old friend, no introduction needed, but it is the first time we meet face to face. And now, I'm fighting not for me but for my baby.

"How bad do you want this baby, Tiff?" it asks. "How long will you suffer for it? How far will you go? How wide? How deep?"

I am pioneering a way for my family tree, here in this bed. This is a marked moment. There is a new line, a new shoot off the family tree. I shake my fist at the future, telling it I will not stop. I will not quit because now I realize it: I want this baby more than I want anything in my life.

This pain has been a constant companion in my life. But here I find something incredible—it is no match for the love that rises up like a warrior in me.

Everything is a blur. The light burns like a stage light as this little one makes its grand entrance of painful separation—the burning of the doctor's fingers running back and forth, stretching my perineum; my whole body pushing; the baby's head tearing through my skin. The last push comes as baby enters into this life, slipping into the hands of the doctor, arms wide in flailing hallelujahs, just like mine were. The doctor tells me it's a girl. I have a daughter. He lays her on my chest; our nakedness touches.

I pull her hands into tiny prayer, quieting her with my love. *Hello, little one. Mommy loves you. You are the prettiest thing I've ever seen.*

She knows me inside out. She instinctively roots around for nourishment, and my tears fall on her head full of matted black curls. I kiss her head, whispering, "We did it, little one." I ask God to help me give her what she needs—help me tend her heart and create a safe home for her. A home that has roots. A home that stays. A mom that stays. A family with a mom and a dad.

I'm opening your eyes in wonder, little one. Heaven's song singing sweet lullabies. Like the rising of the sun, my little love. You too, will always rise. The sun rises suddenly and fiercely. Just like my love for you. Nothing will be too hard for you. I'm making a way for peace to always be your portion. Never forget, little one, I'm traveling with you. You don't go alone. You carry me everywhere. Turn in to me. On the inside. Look for me there. You'll always find me.

I'm remaking you a new tree. Watch me. Its roots wind deep into my earth, wrapping around the ancient rock. Jesus is the Rock.

My words rain down over it all, washing you, cleansing you, and wrapping you in belonging.

Show and tell your Papa-story to your little ones. Feed your babies breadcrumbs. Remember, my candles can't be blown out. My breath brings dead things alive, again and again. There is no "too late" in heaven's language. It isn't in your breath that things live, little one. It's mine. Remember that when it's dark and you can't see.

Little warrior, close your eyes. The more that darkness consumes you, imagine you're a fire, burning bright. My presence is a fire inside you—a fire that not even water can put out.

fifteen

Guilt

Aunt Kathy told me I can't get pregnant while breastfeeding. Still, three months later I am pregnant again. I don't even have my driver's license yet. Ronnie drives me to Grandma's, thirty minutes away, on his way to work.

Grandma drives me to the doctor, and they confirm the positive pregnancy test. We are going to need a bigger place to live. So much for the house I was brought home from the hospital to, Grandpa died in, and the one Ronnie and I made love in for the first time.

On the way home Grandma tells me she can rent out her house in Raytown and move in with us. The next weekend we shop for a new trailer. We find one with a master suite on one end, for Grandma, and two bedrooms on the other. The kids will share a room.

I watch as the semi pulls the new trailer into the lot directly behind our trailer. Maybe God is answering my prayers from the night I ate Ronnie's last supper. He slept and I prayed.

The next month, Grandma gets renters. She moves in with us. In February, Chelsee is born. Twelve days after Nikki's first birthday.

I'm hopeful. We have a new trailer. Grandma helps pay the bills. Ronnie works. Grandma and I raise the girls. We begin living like a real family.

I kiss the girls. Tell them Mommy has to go to work. I leave them with Grandma and Barbara, the teenager up the street. I walk out the door to my other life, the one that doesn't depend on me to hold it together, and I slide into Grandma's blue '77 Monte Carlo in tight jeans and a T-shirt, and as I turn the key, George Michael blares on the radio. I am excited to go to work. At twenty, with two girls under two, this is my first taste of life since marrying and quitting high school.

I work my way through the evening, slicing meat, ringing up customers, scooping ice cream. Sharon, the trailer park gossip who also works with me, and I are doing our closing chores. I feel a guy strutting his stuff in the liquor aisle, copper hair and freckles. He lives a street over from me and is casing my body like a burglar. I pretend not to notice.

He follows me around while I mop. After a few minutes he says, "I like your jeans."

"Thanks," I say.

"What does your boyfriend think about those jeans?"

"I'm married."

"Really?" he says. "That's too bad," he comments, raising his eyebrows.

He wants to talk about sex, like George Michael's song, but I'm not sure I do. I don't think sex is what I'm hungry for. I think I'm hungry for somebody to push through my faux smile, my crippling shyness, the wringing-of-hands awkwardness that keeps me from being known. I don't feel like a girl someone like him would stare at, but his stare wakes something lying dormant, something that's never had a chance to surface. Deep down I know if I want this something-more in my life, I am going to have to find out what it is and go for it.

Weeks into my job, I'm alone at the register, and he asks me if I want to go to his trailer. I mumble something awkward about not being sure, about needing to go home after work. I remember how his eyes make me feel like I am his next victim. But pressured by his presence, I push the thoughts away.

I look to Sharon to tell me what to do. She smiles, nodding her head and giving a wink. I'm scared to call Ronnie and lie, but I do. I tell him I will be late, Sharon and I are grabbing something to eat.

I can't believe I am doing this. It's a risk to see if this is part of the something-more that burns me up. My heart tells me to turn and run. Why don't I listen? He is driving me to his trailer, and I don't feel like this is me sitting here beside him, a stranger. Am I committing a crime entering another woman's bedroom? It feels like it. I fight myself all the way there, smiling to hide the fear of being caught, the fear of being seen. I know God sees me.

We walk past the living room, past his little boy's bedroom, right into their bedroom. I stand there not knowing what I'm sup-posed to do. "I have never done this before," I said. He laughs, a bit drunk at the obviousness of it all, embarrassing me.

I ask myself over and over again what I'm doing. I squeeze my hands over and over, hoping he can't see my skin crawl as his smile turns from flirty to frightening. I have never seen another man naked before, and I watch him undress like he cheats every day. Can he see what we're doing is wrong? This is where his wife sleeps. This is their home, their family, and the pain of that sucks my air out, like I'm dead. Maybe you have to be dead to not feel, to cheat, to break a family up. I take my jeans off, hoping he doesn't see my stretch marks from the two babies I have that are sleeping in their beds across town.

I don't even know you, I say to myself as his body pushes me to his bed. *Am I going to have sex with a stranger in his stranger-wife's bed?*

His hunger is hard and ravenous. His kisses slide around on me like a car out of control. His breath smells like alcohol. I can no longer discern what is making me nauseous. I begin to cry for the wrongness of it all. I cry for my husband, cry for the words I promised at an altar, and I cry for his wife and boys when his touch turns suddenly forcible. I fight the sheets and my disgust to get out of the bed, and his face twists red as his hair. My heart catches the brunt of his anger. His words slap me with the accusation that all my feelings about myself are true.

"What's wrong with you? Leading me on like that? Get out of my house!"

I don't know what I felt the most, the words or my aloneness. Another secret embeds itself in the lining of my heart, shaping the thoughts that fire off in my mind. At home I get in the shower to hide my shame, wash the smell of deception off of my skin, hoping Ronnie doesn't smell it. I did the unforgivable. What crushes women. Crushes families. I have nowhere else to go. No one to talk to. I'm alone.

Less than a week passes, and Sharon tells everyone who will listen at work. She even tells my mom. My mom tells Ronnie. The betrayal leaves me feeling set up, like she sabotaged my happiness, jealous of how much I love being a mom. I want to be home rather than at work. I don't want to be called a cheater.

What do I have to do to pay for cheating? To numb the guilt? To get the smell out? Maybe another baby?

I quit my job and start taking the kids back to church, believing that the more the kids and I are there, the cleaner I will feel. Other than with Grandma, church is the only other place I remember feeling safe. Ronnie doesn't want to talk about what happened, but maybe I'll talk to Brother Don, the preacher, about this something-more buried underneath the smile and the cheating.

But I probably won't.

You don't talk about things like that at church. You can't out your story. Even still, at least in church I am safe. Safe from guys like Eric. Church is where everybody smiles. Smiles cover a multitude of wounds.

The next Sunday, as I stand between Ronnie and Miss Louise, in a dress the color of lilacs, Papa's voice pulls on my heart.

Come, little one, I'm speaking life into you. I know your name. Let me tend to your heart full of cuts, bruises, and welts.

Lean back in my arms. You are not alone. Your name isn't Alone. You are beloved, daughter. A mighty warrior. Be loved by me. I'm right here. Talk with me. I'm listening. I am a safe person. Let me hold the weight, guilt, shame, and the hardness of words that kill your heart. Let me be your soft place to fall. Feel my warmth behind you. I've got your back.

Little one, open your fists. Let me clean you, wash you, my love. My words wash from the top of your head to the bottom of your feet. I'll go deeper still, into your heart, and I will lift it, turning it to me. I don't make bad people good, little one. I take out hearts of stone, give hearts of flesh. Hearts that cry for Papa.

I speak dead things alive. I'm breathing on your heart now, little one. Hold on to me. I've got you. I'm sustaining you. Breathe.

chapter

sixteen

Underneath

leave the girls with Ronnie when I go to the hospital. Grandma is dying. This is the last day I will see Grandma alive. She lays on her side, a fan blowing on her, and she is holding a button she pushes to release morphine into her system. I'm afraid to see her. More, I'm afraid to see through her, to see the fears under her skin. Her fear of dying. She is suffocating from the lung cancer. I can't fix it. I can't make her stay. I can't make her not afraid.

Grandma's fear exposes mine, and it creeps up my back, across the skin on my neck, up my scalp. I can sense it. Will anyone see me anymore when she's gone? Will her death be my own?

I don't know what to say to her. I stand at the end of her bed because looking into each other's eyes would feel too much. There is something holding me back from running to her side and begging her to please not go. I walk out of the room, and as soon as she can't see me, I sob.

In the morning, the phone rings. I know. I answer, listen, and hang up. Grandma is dead. Everything around me keeps moving but me. The room narrows, begins to turn, to flip. The floor is a sea, and I'm sinking in it.

At the funeral, Grandma's three daughters fight over her last wishes, her things, and me. They resent that she loved me, that she wanted me to have her car. I don't want to fight over Grandma's things, her money, or even her car. I'm sad that her death draws out their motives, but I'm also relieved because I know that what I see underneath is real.

I don't go to the viewing of her body, and I stand back from the graveside. I take the whole thing in as a bystander. Grandma isn't here. She is in my blood and in my bones. I wrestle the why, with what's rising up underneath my skin—a cocktail of anger and sadness—as I stand on the edge of the grass, people, and trees. Birds sing like background music. People stand around her coffin, not even in the ground yet. I watch as death disrupts what's under people's skin, telling it to rise up, becoming palpable in their behavior with each other and toward Grandma, who can't defend herself anymore.

I am fighting to take one more breath without letting everyone here see my pain that's like a shovel. I hear the shovel exposing my fears like roots, rocky soil, and hard clay. My fears tell me there's nobody left alive that's safe. Nobody to understand me. All I want to do is let my pain and fears bury me. *I don't know what to do, Grandma! I don't know how the kids and I will make it, how Ronnie will make it. We can't afford a home without you. What's going to happen?*

Grandma died with her pain buried alive inside her. Will I?

Nobody talks about what happens underneath our skin. Sometimes life is an unexposed emergency. Like when a grandma dies and people are ripping apart your life and you can do nothing about it because she isn't your mom, she's your grandma, and there is no safety net to catch you. Sometimes, and often, the other shoe really does fall, and the people that tell you to stop living as if it has have never lived a life of falling shoes. Or if they have, they have forgotten.

I wish people wouldn't forget. Forget that I'm walking behind them. Life can be a hand reaching back, helping, pulling up, if we don't forget.

Maybe I'll be next to descend down into the earth. I feel as if I'm going there now, being buried alive. There is no one left that sees me—not my mom, not Ronnie, and not the kids—and I'm not sure how to hide all of this that's rising inside, all this I'm pushing down with both hands as I try to hold it together.

Nobody can walk us to the other side. Nobody can fix death, not even Grandma. There is nobody left to fix me but me. I have never been alone.

Now that Grandma is gone, I'm sure we'll move in with my mom and stepdad, and I'll start looking for a place to rent that we can afford without Grandma.

Love was snatched away without warning, even though I knew it was coming.

Little one, I see your broken heart. I'm running for you; run to me. My arms are your safety net, catching you. I'm right here all around and inside you.

Little one, my ear is forever on your chest, listening. I specialize in unspoken things. Only I can hear those. Only I can see what lies under skin and gravestones. You aren't crying out to a God who is blind and deaf. I have never left your side, and I won't start today. Your pain doesn't scare me. I'm in it with you, walking with you through every battle. Little one, follow my way. One step. One word. One breath. One hope. One prayer. One moment at a time.

Little one, I've read your story. I know every twist in your story line. I'm outraged at the pain my children cause one another and themselves. I want to help them; I want to help you. Choose me, little one. Choose me. I chose you. Without me, nothing will make sense. Let me help you make sense of Grandma dying. Fear is spinning your world now that Grandma is no longer here, but fear not, I have overcome the world, and that overcoming lives inside you.

Little one, I see you laughing on the other side, where the walls have tumbled and the flowers grow wild.

That's where we are going, together.

Little warrior, let me recover who you are.

seventeen

Words That Kill

We had moved out of the trailer when Grandma went to stay with Aunt Dorothy in Florida. We moved into another trailer before settling into a three-bedroom townhome the next town over. After some months, Grandma had come back, sold her house, and moved back in with us. During that time we had a third baby, a boy named Reece. Four years younger than Chelsee.

I talked to Mom on the phone a few weeks after Grandma died, doing my best to ask for help. What I wanted to say was, whatever it is has been there ever since I can remember. Like a distraction that won't leave me alone. It feels like it takes big bites out of me. Like it is something handed down through my lineage.

I wish I could tell all the secrets in my heart. Then someone could take out a piece of paper and number it, showing me what comes first. Tell me they have a plan for my life. That they will help me do what I can't, until I can. Show me what is mine and what is Ronnie's responsibility.

I knew my words wouldn't come out right. They wouldn't say what I meant. My words would go too deep. It would sound crazy. I've always sounded crazy to Mom. Our dots don't connect.

Instead, I mumbled into the phone. Told her I'm not happy. I don't think I want to be married anymore. When we talk about stuff like this, we agitate each other. I wondered why she seemed so upset with me sharing my heart.

Do I embarrass her? Make her uncomfortable? Or maybe she thinks I'm turning out like her, and that scares her.

"I don't know what to do, Mom," I said.

She told me, "You have kids to think about." She reminded me what a good mother I am for being so young. Told me I was born to be a mother. I've heard this often from people. Those words felt true, but looking at my life, they didn't look true. Something inside me isn't working.

We hung up the phone. Nothing had changed. Only more guilt, shame, and confusion.

Since Grandma died, nothing is making sense.

Ronnie is waiting up for me when I come home from work tonight. I guess he smells the guilt.

He asks, "Are you seeing someone else?"

We haven't been talking much. I know he feels my detachment since Grandma died six months ago. Before she died, I had gone back to get my GED and started college. I was proud of myself for going back and getting my high school diploma after seven years. When I enrolled in college, I felt like I took three big steps toward being an adult. Since she died, I've had to quit college and take a job to make up for her help with the bills.

I close the door behind me and stand there. *Who makes decisions this big? With words?* It has been nine years, and we have no means to keep body and soul together.

My emotions are frail and frightened. My mind is habitually exhausted from rehearsing why our marriage isn't working. Why I'm not working. There is nowhere to put the words that live inside me, so they shoot out of my mouth like a bullet.

"I don't want to be married anymore."

His face goes white.

The words sound like a dead body hitting the floor. My body. His body. I'm not sure. I want to take back everything I said. Try and pretend longer. But there the words lie in the middle of the room. Neither of us move to see if they are still breathing. I think I killed him with my words. Do I hear sirens? If this was a real murder scene, there would be sirens, police, and an ambulance. But it isn't. Maybe it needs to be. But it's too late. Words make people live or make them dead. Tonight it feels like we all died. Words kill. Only you keep on living.

He doesn't offer to get help for us. Or for the kids. Neither do I. He accepts it like pulling the stopper on a bathtub of water. I can almost hear the sound of the last of the water going down the drain.

I can't feel Ronnie's pain right now, or I won't be able to say what I want. I want to find out what this something-more is. Why it won't leave me alone.

We separate our belongings, our hearts, and the kids. I want them. I don't want to separate them. He moves two hours away to live with his parents, who live on land with his grandma. I move into a duplex across the street from the church, next door to the family who babysits the kids.

Oh, sweet one. You have never been more beautiful to me than you are right now. You are safe here with me, darling. Let me hold you together as it feels like your world is crashing down. I love you so . . . shhhh. I'm here. You're safe. The hands that hold the world are holding your children. I've got them. Trust me. I see them. I see Ronnie.

I am bent down with you. I am illuminating the wholeness of my heart for you to see. I am bringing order, giving you nourishment, comforting you. I am raising up my wholeness over you like a wing, tenderly caring for your heart.

I am wallpapering your heart with my love. I am at work night and day to hold your heart. Open your heart to me, my love. You are becoming. I am using everything for your good, little one. I know it doesn't look so now, but remember, my words never come back dead. They go forth making things live. I keep my word. I am who I say I am.

Little one, sometimes I move the mountain, sometimes we go through it, and other times, I throw my lambs up on my shoulders and carry them.

eighteen

What Kind of Mother?

This surviving is different than my surviving before. Then it was me. Now I have three small children, no child support, and am living on a waitress paycheck.

Fear cores my insides out like an apple. I don't have anything or anyone to fill the hole. I can't see what's coming.

Why can't I go somewhere and ask for help? Instead, I sit alone in my duplex. I hear the sound of cars driving by, birds singing, and children playing, evidence that life is able to be lived, yet I look down and all I see is my threadbare skin, my heart protruding—hungry to be loved. I wrap my arms around my knees, pulling them to my chest, doing my best to keep my heart in. To keep it all together.

When the kids are home I pretend the best I can. I don't want them to see me break apart.

I kiss Reece's chubby cheek, breathing him in. He smells like Cheerios from breakfast. How do I tell a one-year-old that Mommy is giving him to Daddy because Mommy isn't safe anymore? How do I tell him I'm getting ready to do something bad? I know it in my guts. I am a semi driving off a cliff.

Later in the week, I hand Reece to Ronnie, with his blanket, hoping it smells like home to him. That it smells like me. I want him to remember me. That I love him. The love and hate in Ronnie's eyes grind me to powder. We both know that later he will drive down and pick up both girls at school, taking them home to live with him. They are safer with Ronnie than me, so I toss them into his life raft and go under, my heavy heart sinking, pulling me to the bottom where I drown in guilt. Shame swallows me whole.

Words haunt me. Mom tells me I'm the weakest of all her children. Grandma says, baby doll, I'm dead, and I can't protect you from bad things anymore. Ronnie almost cries, says he knows he wasn't enough for me. Their words are true. They cut my feet out from under me, and I feel the fear flowing from severed arteries.

I want to ask for help, but I don't. I tell myself I deserve a life of pain for what I've done.

God, where are you? I can't tell.

Brother Don and his secretary bring food for us to make a holiday meal. Food isn't what I need any longer. My need is deeper than food, but what is it? Somebody tell me.

Now I don't see only my pain and other people's pain but also my children's. I try to tell them when they visit on weekends, but I don't know how. So I kiss them, hold them, tell them I love them.

Their body language tells me they carry pain too. I have a family disease, I want to say. It's generational, with no cure, and I gave it to them just like Grandma gave it to Mom and she handed it down to me. Like you pass a dish at a family meal.

What I feared the most has happened. I've become my mom.

I see their faces begging me to come get them as they drive away with their dad after weekend visits, crying faces plastered to the rear window of his Dodge Dakota pickup.

I sob for their fear and what isn't said. *What happened to Mommy? Why are you picking us up? Why are we living here? Do you love us?* I feel their eyes like I feel my own. I feel their bodies for what they can't say. Are they going to freeze in this memory too? What do they think at night when they are in the dark? Do they talk to God like I did?

Stay here, little one. I am waiting to help you. Stay with me in this moment. Don't go to a room in your heart-house alone and shut the door. Breathe. Look up. Do you see the rafters above you holding a canopy of cedar and sweet-smelling pine? This place is ours. Yours and mine. It is our shelter-of-story. This is your safe house inside you. It's Papa country. Smell the fir and fire soaking deep into your memory. To the unknown place before you were born when I held you. Feel it awakening your heart to remember your finding place. Waking up the homing instinct like a tiny bird that I put inside you. I marked you with my love before you were born, like you did with your son, Reece.

The smell of Reece's blanket reminds him of you. My smell, little one, reminds you of me. Of your homeland. Where you come from. Where you're going. What your name is. What your something-more is. I want you to remember me. Remember your homeland.

I am with you in every painful situation. I never turn my back on you. There is nothing you can do to make me love you less, and there is nothing you can do to make me love you more. I will always love you and love you and love you and love you. Remember, you are rooted and grounded in my goodness and kindness. It is the soil I am growing you in.

My love is not passive in your frozenness, in the memory of the ways you've been abandoned. My love is hands-on, kneading in warmth, kindness, and goodness. I am fighting for you. My fierce and fiery love cracking the membrane of ice.

My arm is muscle and my grip is steel, and I am not letting you go. I am for mothers who make difficult choices. I am for you, little one. I am calling you back to put you and your babies together again.

Please listen: keep going. Don't try to push your own heart back in. Don't try to end everything; I want you to know life with me. Let me be your medic. Let me give you my heart-medicine.

This (place) is
ours. Yours and
mine. It is our
shelter-of-story.

—Papa

nineteen

Ice

I t all starts when Rita asks if I want to go ice skating with her this weekend. She suggests I ask Jake to come along too.

Jake, the new guy at work, seems to have the answers to my problems. He is smart, and being with him feels euphoric, but when I'm alone, I feel lost in a new world—a dark, primal jungle. I have no skills to navigate this place.

I can't talk to Jake about it. He doesn't go past the shallows to the deep where I am, where I am not seen. To him, I am a sexual object to be toyed with. Does he see that I have real children? Real pain that is holding me under the water?

"I've been watching Jake flirt with you," she says.

I laugh. He's four years younger than me. "I'm too shy," I say. I try and explain, "When I first saw him coming to work in his letterman's jacket plastered with medals—and he isn't in high school anymore—it was a red flag. He thinks too much of himself. You know, the kind of guy you roll your eyes at because he tries too hard."

But he walks by, smiles with that outgoing fearlessness to live life, and it charms me.

"I'm awkward at stuff like this," I tell her.

Just then Jake walks up behind us. The words stick in my throat. I am nervous around him, like something in him is bigger than me, but his smile melts me, stirs the memory of my stepmom's something bigger. Whatever it is, that feeling, it turns me into a little girl wringing her hands.

"Do you want to go skating with me this weekend?" I ask before thinking it through.

He laughs and asks, "Are you asking me out?"

With just a look, he makes fun of the way I wring my hands. I feel shame laughing at me, turning my face hot, but I push it away because he tells me how cute I am when I "do that thing with my hands." He mimics what I do with my hands. I don't know if he is kidding or not, but I look down and answer.

"Yes, I am."

Jake smiles, says yes, and I can't believe it.

I drive to his house the next Friday night. It had been raining, and it's beginning to snow. I take the back road so I can go slowly. I pull in the drive and he comes out. He wants to take his new red sports car, but I ask if we should still go. It's icy out, the TV says, but he says we will be fine. I don't tell him I'm afraid as we pull out of the driveway. He barely knows me.

I want to tell him to turn around and go back, but I don't. Where is my voice?

We slide around the first corner, and we are not even out of the neighborhood yet. Something inside me shakes when this happens, telling my voice to speak up. Why don't I say stop the car? I want out of here.

We turn onto I-70, speeding up to merge onto the highway. We hit a patch of black ice, and before I know what's happening, we're spinning out of control. Everything happens in slow motion. I see the face of a woman in the car next to us watch as her life flashes before her. She sees my face, we see each other, and then she is gone. We careen into a highway sign, the car forgets gravity and flips, and we roll down the embankment. I grab Jake, pulling him toward me as we spin. I try to save him.

When I come to, I see rows of flashing lights and a paramedic telling me not to move. Blood is all over my sweatshirt, the one I borrowed from my mom. It is her new one that she told me to be careful with. Why is that all I can think about as the paramedic cuts up the arm of my right sleeve? He tells me we were in an accident. I try to see Jake. I look and see he is in pain, telling them he wants his mom. I'm sitting right next to him when he says that, and for some reason it hurts me.

The paramedic tells me we T-boned a highway sign on Jake's side of the car, flipping us before we rolled down the embankment. We are lucky to be alive, he says. They tell Jake to be still and they will have him out soon. His side of the car is smashed in on him. Paramedics tell us they're bringing the Jaws of Life to cut Jake out.

Different ambulances take us to separate hospitals. They say I hit my head into the window, so they stitch it up and have to keep me overnight to watch for signs of a concussion. I ask the nurses if they know anything about Jake. They tell me he fractured his hip but he will be okay. They also called my mom, they say.

They release me the next day and Jake a few days later. He is on crutches and bed rest when I bring him something to eat. He tells me how I saved his life, how they said he wouldn't have been so lucky if I hadn't pulled him to me. The guardrail would have crushed his whole left side. He tells me he's okay, though, even asks for sex, though his hip is fractured.

Do you love me now? I want to say. I want to know.

I stay a few days to take care of him. We lay in bed most of the time since he is on bed rest and crutches. There he tells me I am everything he prayed for in a wife. He tells me he used to go to church with his high school sweetheart. Her dad was the pastor. He was like a dad to Jake, given the fact that his own dad had a drinking, lying, and cheating problem. His mom kicked his dad out, divorced him, and took three jobs to support the kids. And the whole time his only role model had been that preacher who tried to tell Jake about God. My insides perk up when he says God. I want someone who talks about God.

He has never told me anything deep about himself before. I feel closer to him now. Maybe this is it. The one God has for me. Maybe we can make a home, have our own kids, and sit around the dinner table and talk about God.

He informs me that he only tells his mom he loves her. Do I have to be his mom to be told I am loved? Am I his mom? Maybe I am his mother supply. I can't mother my children, but maybe I can mother him; maybe myself too? I read once of a cardinal rule: don't get high on your own supply. If I mother us, I will have none left to mother my own children.

From then on, I bring him food and give him good, good love, just like that song by Tesla.

My love is here for you, always. I will never break your heart. My words are like healing ointment, making your heart whole and healthy, healing your heart piece by wounded piece. My words are unearthing your heart, unlocking your surrender—your *yes* to being seen, known, and found. My words don't stop there, little one. They walk with you as you learn to steward the wholeness I'm bringing you. They grow you up all the way home.

Jesus blessed and broke his body, passing it around as bread, multiplying it so that your heart doesn't have to be broken, passed around, and eaten. You will learn that you will have excess as you take and eat my breadcrumbs. They will fill you, overflowing. You will give from the fullness I am imparting to you. Not from your heart. From my heart.

I restore what was lost. I gave the world Jesus, so that you could be safe and spared. You don't have to be punished. The debt has already been paid. Come home. Come to my table, child. It's time to eat. The dinner bell is ringing. My bread puts strength in your bones and honey in your veins. Let me pull you up to my table and nourish your starving heart.

Come home. Come to my table, child. It's time to eat. The dinner bell is ringing. My bread puts strength in your bones and honey in your veins.

—Papa

chapter

twenty

Sleeping Pills

We make out on the living room floor. My hands are on his biceps.

I can't believe his muscles. "I've never had a man with muscles," I say without thinking. He laughs. Stupid turns my face red.

I squeeze my eyes shut, letting the words *I love you* form in my mind before saying them, then I whisper them. I hold my breath, waiting for what he will say. Will he laugh at me? In that moment, I let him hold my life in his hands, give him the power to crush it with one word.

He looks at me, his face like stone, and reminds me, "I don't tell anyone I love them except my mom." He laughs.

What do I do with that? Maybe I shouldn't have put him in that position. After all, what kind of girl says what's in her heart? I sit here smiling awkwardly, fumbling for something to fill the agonizing pause in the air, but his words have taken my heart by the feet and swung it around wildly. Then there's panic. I want to pull the words back, or rewind the tape, or else die right here in front of him. I want to get on my knees and beg him to forget it. I want him to stay.

He gets up and walks to the door. *Say you love me,* I plead silently. *I'll do anything if you will stay.*

He smiles and walks to his car. He pulls out of the drive.

When he slips out of sight, my mind begins to think up a plan to fix what I just ruined with three words. I don't know why taking pills comes to mind, but it does. I argue with myself but I don't listen. I will myself to turn off my thoughts, to not feel.

I drive to the convenience store up the street where I used to work and buy a bottle of sleeping pills. I call him from the pay phone, tell him I took a bottle of sleeping pills, hoping he will come. He's says, "That's crazy." I know it's crazy, but desperation drags me down. I hang up the phone. I get in the car, adrenaline pumping and building the courage to actually do it. I drive back to my duplex, open the box, and take the whole bottle. Just like that. I lock the door and sit in the dark.

Jake doesn't come; the fire department does. I see flashing lights, followed by a knock on the door. I don't answer it. I'm scared. They go around back, try the door, then go back to the front, knocking so loudly I think they might break it down, so I answer it. The firefighter tells me they got a 9-1-1 phone call that I had taken sleeping pills.

I lie, saying I didn't. He says if they have to come back out, they won't be happy. Then he leaves.

What did I do? Why did I send them away? Do I really want to die?

I see flickering lights in front of me, and they aren't from a fire truck. They just float in the air. Terror runs me to the neighbors. I tell them I took a bottle of sleeping pills and am seeing things.

They call 9-1-1 again. I sit in their chair, wanting to just sleep as we wait for help to come. Life slows down to only snapshots. Every time they wake me up I see another scene. The neighbor on the phone is taking direction from the operator to keep me awake. Paramedics enter. I see their lips moving, but they're all on mute. I watch them find a vein. I'm stupid and in trouble. I'm a child, with their sorry looks scolding me for lying. This is what asking for help looks like, feels like, when you call 9-1-1.

I ask the paramedic when they are rolling me onto the ambulance if I am going to die. He smiles then, saying, "No, we got you."

I turn my head and see the neighbors—including church family neighbors—watching me. They must be telling each other what a bad mother I am and discussing how I might die. When you sin, when you leave your children, you deserve this kind of thing, one of them says, or at least that's what I imagine her saying. It's sad, the father says, head shaking, finger pointing. I don't feel their words though. I don't feel anything, really. Finally.

I wake up with a tube down my throat. The flavor of charcoal and bile is thick as my stomach is pumped. I am in the hospital under surveillance. Jake had come to the hospital, Mom tells me, but she told him to stay away from me. She told him it was his fault I took the pills. She blamed him, and I blame her for ruining all of this for me. Now Jake will never come back, and I'll never be able to explain how I just want him to pay attention. I am not only someone to have sex with. I am a real girl.

Brother Don comes to visit me. Someone, probably the neighbors, told him about my stupid stunt. He sees that I'm afraid and asks me what happened and listens to what I'm not able to put into words.

He asks if I love Jake. I say I do. He sits with me in my overdose. He doesn't tell me I am wrong for loving Jake. He doesn't scold me, doesn't tell me I'm wrong for taking all those pills. I already know I'm stupid. At least that's how I feel. Maybe Brother Don knows that sitting with me as my inner and outer world are shattering and saying nothing is the greatest kindness of all. His silence fills me with hope. Maybe Brother Don is for me.

The doctors and nurses and Mom want to keep me under watch and give me medicine, but I tell them what they want to hear. I promise to get counseling.

I am released into Mom's care. She takes me back to the trailer park. I spend the night, but depression, memories, and smells suffocate me here. I need to be with Jake, trying to talk this out. I know he thinks I'm crazy now.

I break my promise to go to counseling, exchanging it for a six-pack of beer. I laugh because I've never been a drinker, but tonight I do. Maybe if I drink enough I won't care that Jake doesn't love me or that I'm stupid.

It's dark; the only light streams in from the front window. My heat has been shut off, and I can't keep warm by the little space heater in the living room. There's nothing here but a mattress, a space heater, a phone, and the darkness. I stare at the phone, begging it to ring. Begging for Jake to call, but he doesn't. I listen to sad love songs to follow the beer. It's midnight and my feelings are drunk. I pick up the phone and call.

He answers. He sounds sympathetic, asking me if I'm alone. I say yes.

He says, "I'm coming over."

He knocks and enters, bringing me a portable heater for my bedroom. We get in bed. He covers me up. Tells me I'm okay. When he's here I'm not alone. Maybe he can stand in front of me to take the brunt of what's coming. Maybe it doesn't matter that he doesn't love me, at least that's what I tell myself. I wonder what I will have to give to be loved by him.

My love, I want to rescue you, not punish you. I want you to live, not die. Little one, you believe that you're nothing without someone else. You are like a million pieces all floating aimlessly, with only skin keeping them together. How can a human, someone made of dust like you, hold those pieces together? Only I can. You risk everything for that someone else—home, family, and now your kids and your life. Is it working? Risk giving me everything. Risk your life on me, little one. I am a sure thing.

Turn around and come to me. Let me give you a bone-deep hug. I love you, little one. My heart hurts with you, for you. Let me put your pieces back together. Let me give you wholeness, piece by piece. Let me keep it all together. Then follow me to the table and we'll sit together, just the two of us. At the table I will awaken your heart. At the table I will help you grow up. I will give you direction. I will teach you how to live loved. I will show you how. I am transforming you into my beautiful bride. I am writing a real-life, true fairy tale. Your fairy tale, my love. One day soon, you will stand mature and faithful in the day of battle. Not overcome in it. Keep taking the next step you know to take, my love. Keep doing the next right thing. I'm cheering you on.

chapter

twenty-one

Send Me

I have spent all my life hungry. The compulsion to drink the depths of life like an ocean went out with the tide and washed up a hunger to take in the Word of God. I didn't do anything to get this new hunger. It lies within me like a seashell, waiting to be picked up.

This is how I remember it beginning.

I notice it when a new youth pastor comes and preaches from the old book, and then more as I go through a Bible study and find these words coming alive to me, breadcrumbs leading someplace bright.

I find I want more. I find spending time with his words leads me to God himself. The words are more than words though. Like ink spilled on wet paper, they get absorbed and spread. That's what the words must do. Slowly, ever so slowly, his words bleed into my heart, then out from my heart, into my everyday, ordinary life.

I begin—not even consciously—hungering for things I never did before. Without trying. Instead of waking up in the mornings to get the kids and I ready and getting housework and dinner started, I want to learn what God is like. Who he is. I want to talk to him, and I want him to talk to me. So I make time for that by getting up before everyone else.

New life intersects for me in this small rural town in Missouri, where God's words find me, and I am awake to them. This waking is like coming out of anesthesia, like rising after a long sleep.

It doesn't take long for me to sense my taste buds changing. I don't want the comforts I wanted before; now I crave these words that fill me in a way I'd not known was possible.

Then my thought patterns begin to change as well. I begin to rearrange my life to position my cold heart next to God's campfire. I can suddenly see habits in my life that I knew God was gently calling me away from. Slowly, he begins melting my heart, changing me from the inside out. It isn't anything drastic all at one time. Rather, it is slow interior work, invisible work, what Eugene Peterson calls "a long obedience in the same direction."

We all want outward, immediate change. But this is slow work on the inside, sacred work. But I can feel it taking root, and soon others start to see it too.

The pastor asks me if I would like to help with Vacation Bible School, then if I would help teach a single women's Sunday school class. I begin to harbor this love of studying the Bible and sparking this love in others.

I love seeing the women's eyes light up when God shows them something they hadn't seen before. I love letting them know how much he loves them. There are all kinds of single women. Divorced, mostly. Some have little children, some have grown children, and one is a war veteran who lives her life in a wheelchair. All of us are hungry for holy words.

When I read, eat, and act on words from the Bible, they go down deep into my insides, penetrating my surface superficiality, my negative narratives, all the way down to the deepest dark, secret places.

When I read the Bible, the words burn deep inside me. They alleviate the ache. When I spend time reading them and talking to God, I don't want to play it safe. Something in me wants to come out and do something brave, and it scares me.

The girls live with Jake and I now, while Reece stays with his dad.

We live across the street from this church. The church yard and our yard are only separated by a neighborhood street. We walk to church three times a week.

Pastor Jedidiah, our youth pastor, is an answer to my year of begging God to bring someone to the church to help me. He's proof that God sees me, hears me. He and his wife and children are staying on campus at Midwestern Baptist Theological Seminary. They came all the way from St. Kitts to a small rural town in Missouri. Our tiny church hired him as our youth pastor at the pastor's recommendation. They are a black family in an all-white church. I can stick my hand in the water and feel the coolness of the current when he stands up to preach for the first time.

I am sitting in my usual third row pew, full of expectation, like I am pulling up a chair to the best meal I've ever had. He stands up, opens to Isaiah 6 (MSG), and simply reads word for word:

In the year that King Uzziah died, I saw the Master sitting on a throne—high, exalted!—and the train of his robes filled the Temple. Angel-seraphs hovered above him, each with six wings.

With two wings they covered their faces, with two their feet, and with two they flew. And they called back and forth one to the other,

Holy, Holy, Holy is God-of-the-Angel-Armies.
His bright glory fills the whole earth.

The foundations trembled at the sound of the angel voices, and then the whole house filled with smoke. I said,

Doom! It's Doomsday!
I'm as good as dead!
Every word I've ever spoken is tainted—
blasphemous even!
And the people I live with talk the same way,
using words that corrupt and desecrate.
And here I've looked God in the face!
The King! God-of-the-Angel-Armies!"

Jedidiah continues reading:

Then one of the angel-seraphs flew to me. He held a live coal that he had taken with tongs from the altar. He touched my mouth with the coal and said,

"Look. This coal has touched your lips.
Gone your guilt,
Your sins wiped out."

And then I heard the voice of the Master:

   "Whom shall I send?

   Who will go for us?"

I spoke up,

   "I'll go.

   Send me!"

Jedidiah's accent makes the words all the more beautiful. The words begin connecting dots in my heart. Papa is writing my story! But it's bigger than me. I see it is for others too. I haven't been on my own! He's found me! He picks me up and carries me to his table. I don't have to do anything but let him. He is more than a spectator over my life; he wants to get inside my life. Inside me. He wants me to experience him.

It feels like God pulls out a chair for me to sit down. He breaks off bread and says open your mouth, my love. I want to give you food for your heart.

I am surprised. Words, like honey, make their way over my palate. Slow and sticky. All the way down to that hollow ache. I am tasting things I have no language for.

I begin to weep. I can't hide the sound, so I muffle my mouth with my hands as my body is wracked with sobs. God is real. He sees me. And he wants to help. He wants to tell me what happened to me. Why I hurt inside. All eyes are looking at me, and I try to quiet the voice in my head telling me I'm embarrassing myself, but I can't stop crying. I need these words, this food for my soul. I've been so hungry for so long.

"Who will go for me?" Jedidiah reads, and my hand shoots up.

"Yes, send me!"

I feel exposed, but for the first time, I don't hurt.

When I leave church, I know I have heard God's voice deep in the center of me. He fought for me there. He set a table for me there. He fed me there.

It is a safe place.

You're thirsty, gulping words like water, letting it spill out of the edges of your lips, but you don't care. This is the medicine, little one. This is what you've been searching for since the beginning. You've been drinking polluted water, trying to quench your thirst, trying to be made well, but it doesn't satisfy, nourish, or restore.

There's more to life with me than a simple sinner's prayer or walking down an aisle. Little one, soon my words will find you and gather you up. My words will be your map, leading you to Papa's heart.

Little one, when you go where I send you, you will speak what I feed you. You will keep reading Isaiah 6 and what he is to say to the hearts of my people. There is so much more ahead for you. I will lead you. I will not leave you or turn my back on you. I'm not going anywhere. Ever. I am leading you into the wilderness where I will awaken your heart to my love. I will use circumstances, affliction, adversity, and yes, even the enemy to knead the orphan out of you. I am remaking you into my daughter. I am calling up the beloved warrior buried inside you. Watch—she is about to rise.

twenty-two

The First *Rhema* God Speaks

My alarm goes off at 4:00 a.m. It's been some weeks since Jedidiah preached those words, and I want more. I had set the alarm earlier, hoping to get up before Jake. But no matter how early I set it, he follows. I want to be alone with God, I tell him. He doesn't like that.

Most mornings, he walks out and tells me to come back to bed. He tells me he wants to be together. I want to stand up and yell, leave me alone! Let me be with God! But most mornings, I follow him back to bed.

This morning, though, he doesn't come, and I find my safe place, my table alone with God. He feeds me here in the quiet. Just enough for today.

I'm fasting for the first time. I am reading a book Jedidiah gave me on the spiritual discipline—a lost art he says. Jesus's followers fasted. So did Jesus. Jedidiah tells me fasting seeks to take hunger pains and exchanges them for longing for a greater taste of Jesus.

Today, instead of eating peanut butter toast, I'm eating Isaiah.

As I sit here reading, words begin swimming around on the page. I blink to focus them. It's as if these words are the courses of a meal coming together at the table. It's as if they're meant for me to take and eat, so I do. For the first time, I leave a table full, more than full.

There is a lingering longing. An aftertaste. I don't know whom to tell about what just happened. I date these words in my Bible to mark this moment that I want to remember for a long time to come.

This is your something-more, little one. Me, my words, and your reason for being born. They fill you full and leave you hungrier than ever. In the best possible way. They've always been here, but now you've found them. Eat, drink, until you are full. My words are a never-ending supply of the best food you've ever eaten.

You were born to eat heaven's bread, broken open words.

This book, my story, is taking you somewhere. My words finally found you; you see them, hear them, feel them, taste them. They are strengthening your spine. Now you sense what has always been true: my words are the center of your being. Let them breathe life back into you.

I will wage war against those who wage war against you, who push against what my words say.

And just so you know, I didn't create you to fit in, to belong. Not in this world. Nowhere in my words does it tell you that. That is not my voice. Earth's words are not your native language. Earth's food is not your native food. My words are. That's why you feel so moved, so full.

twenty-three

Come in
the Water

Jake and I felt our family was complete after having our son, Dakota. Dakota was number four for me, but Jedidiah suggested to Jake and I to have another baby. I said no at first. But something in me lingered on the idea, so I prayed. I asked God to change my heart if it was him. And he did. After a few months of charting my temperature daily, checking for ovulation, praying like Hannah, and believing for a girl, we were pregnant.

The late July heat has me wanting to chew someone's head off. Fifth pregnancies can do that to you. I suffer with severe morning sickness the first trimester.

My pregnant state keeps me antsy in the pews, but church feels familiar and routine. We grab our hymnals and turn to page forty.

Brother Rick reads the announcements: there is a potluck after the service and volunteers are needed for nursery duty. The pastor preaches while watching the clock because we all know that today there is a potluck. He stops ten minutes earlier than other Sundays. We stand and sing as the altar opens for anyone who wants to get saved. Sunday after Sunday it's no different. Today, Miss Willa plays "Just as I Am." Again.

Eating God's Word, talking to him, and listening for his voice are how I am discovering who he is. What he's like. Nothing about it is familiar, routine, or lifeless.

I sigh. *God, where are you in all of this?* My heart throws its arms up, wide and wild. This church service is something *we* are doing. This doesn't feel like God initiating anything. Doesn't feel like we are following Jesus. It feels like we are following religion, rules, maybe a deacon board.

A good altar call is like a game of Duck, Duck, Goose. Papa walks round and round and around. I've already walked the aisle. I've said the sinner's prayer. The secretary even added a number to the board in the back of the church when I moved my membership from Bates City Baptist to here. I wonder whom Papa will choose today, if anyone; it doesn't happen often.

I am not anticipating anything when the song begins to sound funny. Words cut in and out. Words I know. We sing them every Sunday.

Blood was shed for me. Come. Wait not. Cleanse each spot. Tossed about. Conflict, doubt, fighting fears, within and without. All I need is Thee. Welcome. Pardon. Cleanse. Relieve. Because of thy promise I believe. Broken every barrier down. Come.

Papa's hand taps my head. *You're it*, he says. *Come in the water.* My heart beats out of my chest. Today? Now? Despite everything, he's laid his hand on my head right in the middle of the line "just come as you are."

In that moment, I understand. I hear. Papa says he wants to feed me, just like Jesus fed the disciples at the Last Supper. He tells me familiarity, routine, people, rules, or even deacon boards can't keep him from acting.

I initiate, little one. I move people and things.

God, I was born hungry. Nothing satisfies me like you do. I seem to live aware of you more and more. But I am nine months pregnant with Grace, my fifth child, swollen to the point I can only wear Nike flip-flops, and you're asking me to walk an aisle and stand up front to get baptized?

But the water seems to call, saying "Come, drink, and you will never thirst again." I believe that.

So I walk the aisle to the water.

I feel Papa's assurance that a new journey has begun.

Pastor Tim asks me if now is a good time to be baptized or if I want to wait until after I have baby Grace. I don't want to wait. I'm ready.

Pastor Tim says a quick prayer.

I step into the water thinking, *This isn't about becoming a member of a building or saying a sinner's prayer. This is about obedience, isn't it, Papa?*

Yes, little one. Keep going.

So I do.

And though the water itself isn't anything special, I sense the water facilitating the exchange. It's gospel-rich water, full of spiritual nutrients, like a mother's womb. And in my spirit, I feel God giving more of himself to me.

I come out of the water not thirsty, not hungry. I see with new eyes. I know now that I am raised up new, the mother of a new genealogy, a line of risk takers, game changers, light bringers, generational wrecking balls, home builders, yes sayers, Red Sea walkers, kingdom of darkness topplers, audacious pioneers, and intrepid explorers.

My family tree goes through the cross, Papa whispers, *and so does yours. Your identity is etched in wood and the Word.*

The Holy Spirit moves like the wind in the trees. We can't see it or control it. It disrupts agendas. I didn't do anything to make it happen. What I did have was a choice when it found me: to reach out and catch Papa's words, or not. Whether I understood it or not. Sometimes understanding comes after the yes. Sometimes it comes years later. And sometimes it comes once we're home.

Daughter, you see it now, don't you? You are wide-awake on the inside, well fed. Let me keep feeding you in a way no one else can. I always keep a careful eye on you. I am delivering you, little one. Out of bondage from cruel taskmasters. They're not only other people, little one; these enemies live inside you too. I am leading you in the wilderness. It's an expedition from fear to freedom, a journey to wholeheartedness, a pilgrimage of growing in love. I'm feeding you breadcrumbs. Just enough for the day. I will go before and behind you, wrapped all around you. Let me take your hands and lead you.

My family tree goes through the cross, and so does yours. Your identity is etched in WOOD AND THE Word.

—Papa

That something inside you that's always been there, that homing instinct, has led you back home. To me. To your finding place. The only way to become what you're meant to be, little one, is for the old you to die. Your heart, hunger, and habits. So I can raise the new you up. My beloved warrior. My partner for life. It's who you are meant to be. I am bringing you out into a wilderness. Training you. Teaching you to fight fair and well so that when we enter your new land you will know how to stand and fight. Listen and act. Eat the breadcrumbs; they are my gift to you. Learn how to wield my words like a sword. Little one, follow me, and I will show you your place in my story.

Reach out. Take and eat.

chapter

twenty-four

Safe

spend too much time trying to connect the dots. My mom. My
husband. My church. How do they connect? The end result is a
triangle. I call them the trinity. Three places people need to feel
safe: parents, marriage, and church. I remember a couple at church
talking about a counseling place that's not too far away. It is a good
place, they said.

I ask Nikki, now fourteen, and Chelsee, thirteen, to put Grace in
her car seat. I ask Dakota, now five, to grab some toys, and I grab
the diaper bag, and we load up the Jeep Cherokee to drive us to the
counseling place. I tell the girls to watch the little ones so I can run in.
I feel like the addict who is crashing, needing a line, but also like I am
the line, like someone else is waiting to use me. I'm the one being used
in my home, but who will ever believe this? Most days I don't believe it.

I sneak in the door to the counselor's office like I'm cheating, or
maybe like I am breaking the law, Jake's law. *I don't sneak well and
seem to get caught in the littlest things*, I think as I step inside.

The receptionist asks me a loaded question.

"Can I help you?"

I don't know if anybody can help me, but I don't dare tell her this. I don't think anyone can handle real truth. Does she really want to know?

I don't think we can afford this kind of help. I don't have access to money. Jake questions every dime I spend. Besides, I can't find one word to tell her what I need. The words freeze midthought. I don't know what I need. I try to get the words together while I glance at the books on a table. She tells me the books are for sale if I see anything that interests me.

I take the books off the shelf, skimming through them. They say things I've never seen anywhere else before. I read about circles of responsibility, religious and spiritual abuse, unhealthy anger and biblical patterns for reconciliation, forgiveness, even restoring lost identity. I'm not sure what any of it means, but my breath catches when I read how God only gives grace for truth. What does that mean? I don't know but I want to find out.

The books tell stories that sound like Jake and me. They sound like what goes on behind closed doors at home. They talk about things my church won't talk about. I buy them and ask her how much it costs to see a counselor. She tells me, and I'm not sure how I can afford that. How can I hide it from Jake? How can I even hide the books from him?

And I thought I was the only one. Maybe I'm not. I sense a breadcrumb. Maybe it will lead somewhere. I know it is from God. Nobody tells me this. But I know. So I take and eat.

On Sunday, Jedidiah tells me he's taking the youth to Texas for a Passion Conference and asks if Jake and I would like to go as chaperones. Jake is excited. We say yes.

Between conference sessions, we stay in a motel, with our doors opening to the outside. I share a room with a group of junior high girls, and Jake shares with the junior high boys. After lights-out, Jake knocks on my door. I step outside and close the door. He begins harassing me, telling me he is divorcing me. I am caught off guard, not knowing what brought this on. He's jealous that the pastor is hanging around our family a lot. Maybe jealous of God too. He says he feels like they are taking his family away. I begin to panic that someone will hear. I ask him to please stop. I walk down to the corner, away from my room where the youth girls—including my own girls—are sleeping. "You're scaring me," I say. This is a youth trip I tell him. This is about God, not us.

Jedidiah comes out of his hotel room and walks toward us, silencing our argument. It's as if someone told him I needed help. Instantly, I can breathe.

"Hello," he says. "Everything okay?"

"Yes," I smile, hiding tension mixed with relief as Jake goes back to his room and I to mine.

Jake wakes me up just after I have fallen asleep. He hisses in my ear, telling me I'm not a godly wife if I don't submit to his need for sex.

"If you don't want sex with me, then who are you giving it too?" he asks. "Who are you with?"

The interrogation goes on for a few hours. I am trapped, so I roll into a fetal position with my hands over my ears, but it isn't enough. I still hear his shaming words. I still hear his breath in my ear, and I can still hear his voice over the screams in my head.

I'm tired, unable to sleep. I take in his words and begin to doubt myself. *Am I not a godly wife? Am I supposed to give him everything all the time?*

I'm suffocating in bed, but just before I spill over the edge of sanity, he gets quiet. I can breathe. I am spent, but just before I fall back to sleep, he starts all over again. He tells me I'm not submitting to him. That godly wives have sex and don't deny their husbands. He accuses me of cheating again. I tell him I'm not cheating with anyone. *No one, except maybe God,* I think. Can someone be jealous of someone's relationship with God?

I listen and listen to Jake all night, and by the morning, I hate him. He doesn't want anyone to know. He tells me this at breakfast, tells me I'd better keep my mouth shut.

I am silenced. I am invisible. No one can see the abuse. Except my children and God. There are no blows to leave bruises on my skin, just wounds on my heart.

I ask God why I've been so weak. Why had I let him back in? When I asked him to leave, there was no help for the in-between. We separated with no plan. It felt more chaotic than before. I have no job, no money of my own, no safety net.

I know there is a plan for marriage—God's plan—but nobody, including our church, knows what that is. The church we are at tells the woman to submit to the man. There is no help for us.

The abuse is trapped under my skin, I tell Papa. *It can't be proven when you can't see it. If he hit me, then I'd have proof. How many years can this go on before I die alive?* I sense Papa pull me close.

You are not invisible or an inanimate object, little one. I see you. People cannot see motives; only I can. I see through skin and bone. I am the only one who can x-ray hearts and see motives. I see your heart—bleeding, bruised, and broken, begging me to heal it. I see your brokenness; I see what's missing. I can give you things in exchange for what isn't working. Things like love, intimacy, good bread. Things only I can give. Things that make your heart whole.

Submitting to sex, to abuse, is not godliness, little one. When any man says as much, I roar like a lion. I am not behind this coercion. I want to help the abused. Let me tend and mend the wounds of abuse, even the invisible ones.

Look up to me. Listen to my voice, and I will navigate you to safety. To a safe house. A safe bed. A safe table.

twenty-five

Red Flag

Jake and I are separated. Again. He came to visit a few nights ago, and I wouldn't open the door until he agreed to come to counseling with me. He cried, said he missed me and was sorry, and gave me flowers. I believe he is telling the truth. This time.

We're in counseling now, and my red flag is up. I know this isn't safe. The counselor's eyes send me signals. Unsettle me. I can't get comfortable in the chair. I don't know why. Until he tells me in front of Jake that I need to stay in the marriage. We don't get to much of anything else. I break down sobbing, and he says, "Why does this upset you?" The mocking misogyny in his voice makes my skin crawl.

Jake stares at me as if to say I told you so. It is your fault. You do need to submit to me.

The questions push me against the wall. I slide down slowly until the questions pin me to the ground. Interrogate me. Confuse me. Is it God or the enemy speaking through the counselor?

As the counselor talks, I'm almost convinced that I am to submit to Jake sexually. I'm to do what he says. If I don't, maybe I'm not a godly wife. Maybe God is punishing me. Maybe I deserve this. I chose it. Isn't God punishing me for giving my children away? For getting divorced and not going to church and not giving everything we have to their building and activities?

By the time the hour is up, my spine has shrunk to half its size. I'm on the brink of despair, then I hear: *You are not wrong, the counselor is.*

I drum up the courage to call the counseling center later in the week. I ask if there is someone else I can see, and they introduce me to Shelia. They tell me that the other counselor is no longer there. I'm relieved. Sheila hears me, and so does the founder of the place and author of all those books on the front table, Chuck Lynch. Shelia tells me they are familiar with narcissistic abuse, a term I've never heard before. They diagnose me as codependent, an enabler, and a victim. They tell me we are a dysfunctional family. Name tags can pin you down and never let you get up again. They put you in your place. They rename you permanently, with no hope of getting a new one. I see Shelia alone for a few months. Jake sees Chuck a few times. We meet once with the kids. Chuck tries explaining that our church's teachings are disordered. Maybe even the gospel is distorted. There is more than one cycle of abuse going on, but it's too late. Our family is battered, broken.

The girls are now in junior high and are eyewitnesses to our story. I'm painfully aware that they see what is happening. That it is shaping them too. We talk about our secret life, the one nobody will believe if we tell them. What a happy, loving family we look like from the outside. I tell them everything God is doing inside me.

I tell them the truth. Even truth about me. I tell them I'm taking God at his words. That I'm doing something with the little I'm learning. That I'm not just hearing God's words; I'm doing them. Even in this hard place. I tell them we have hope. I tell them these are the words I'm holding on to today.

Am I a God anyone can hide from? Do I not see what happens in secret? Am I not everywhere, filling heaven and earth? I see the whole picture. I see what is being done. I see the something bigger that is happening in and to the both of you, your marriage, and your family. I am for family, not abuse. Not physical, spiritual, or emotional abuse.

Beautiful one, you ravish me with your pursuit of me. You're reaching for me even in the dark, my love. My arm is not too short that it cannot save. Little one, stay close behind me. I'm leading the way. I'm working against every enemy attack and making you strong in the feet to stand up against him. I am setting courage and strength in your heart, setting your heart on a steadfast pilgrimage of turnaround.

One day you will not shrink back from your call, but in holy hardness of endurance, you will turn to it with your whole heart. You will live unafraid as my messenger. My love, sound the alarm, tell our story. Tell it in such a way that every drop of Jesus blood makes the enemy pay.

chapter

twenty-six

Safety Net

I go to counseling teachable. I know I need help. I've been begging for it my whole life. Finding a safe place to speak my truth feels like the last and only option. I remember very well what tearing a family apart feels like, and I don't want the kids to go through that. I don't want to go through that again. I love Jake and I hate him all at the same time. I'm also committed to my marriage even if Jake isn't, aren't I? Even if he insists on abuse.

I tell the counselor the way I love Jake feels different. It's less like love and more like dependency. I am addicted to him, and I'm also the addict's supply. I can't seem to quit him, I tell her. He says he'll kill himself if I leave him. He'll even take away all my money. I don't have any other source of income. I haven't worked in years. Four of my five children live with me, and I'm homeschooling them.

We go to counseling separately and together. Jake talks with Chuck. I talk with Shelia.

When Shelia and I are alone, she tells me she sees past Jake's surface. When we are all in the room together, I watch, and if he is questioned long enough, cracks begin to show. They catch him in lies. They see a bit of what I see at home.

When it is Shelia and I, she tells me I'm not crazy and that the illusion I was living isn't reality. I don't believe it at first. Sheila, who is a woman I feel safe with, sends me home with books about marriages like ours. Books titled *Men Who Hate Women and the Women Who Love Them* and *Fool-Proofing Your Life*.

She tells me it takes skilled counselors to spot this type of abuse. It is the first time *ever* that I feel seen, heard, and validated in my marriage.

I tell her he is so good at hiding the abuse that nobody will ever believe me. Most days I don't believe me. She tells me it doesn't matter that nobody else understands or believes me. She tells me I need to be in a safe place and so do my kids, that it isn't a good idea to have let him back in so soon. It makes it harder to get him back out.

I tell her I'm broken, that there is something that needs to be put back together in me. I tell her I feel like a little girl inside. That Jake acts like a father. I have to do what he says. She tells me there is hope for me, that I'm worth the time. She promises there's a hand reaching down to pull me out of the water like a drowning victim.

Shelia pulls me in for a hug, tells me, "God understands, Tiff. He does. His words are his hands; take his hand. Take him at his words. He is fighting for you. He will not fail. He knows the way." She gives me another squeeze.

I try practicing some of the tools I'm learning at the counseling center, but tables keep turning, shoes keep dropping.

Shelia doesn't know I'll let Jake back in before he makes long-term changes. Before he earns back my trust. Before he establishes ongoing accountability. I don't have any income. I am at his mercy. I am out of options. The kids and I do not have a safety net of people to catch us and carry us. The kids and I become our own safety net.

Grab my gospel with both hands, little one. It is your life preserver. It'll keep you afloat, even when you choose the troubled waters. Even when you're out of human options. Remember, I am not human. Even the wind and waves know the sound of my voice.

Reach for me. Even now I am creating a human safety net for you. You wouldn't believe it if I told you. They will catch you, help you, travel with you. Something like family. That is what my church is meant to be. A family. I have a new beginning for you. An inheritance. I am far down the road, working. Even though your eyes can't see it yet. Think back over what you know of me so far. I will not let you down. I keep my word. Take my words like a walking stick. We are on a pilgrimage, caravanning our way home. With each step toward home, my Word is pulling you into my story.

You believe life is a bully and you are without a choice except to be beaten down by it. You believe it holds you under, steals your air. You believe it starves you. These are lies. You're my daughter. You are my beloved warrior, and no one can say otherwise. Only I have the last word, and it is this: you are strong. I will use all of your life to teach you that you do have a choice. You can accept the invitation to be saved from drowning. You can accept the invitation to have your feet set on dry ground. You can accept the invitation to my table. I'll feed you. Let me.

Grab my gospel with both hands,

little one. It is your life preserver.

It'll keep you afloat,

even when you choose the

troubled waters.

—Papa

chapter
twenty-seven

Mirrors

I wipe the fog from the bathroom mirror like I wish I could wipe the self-loathing off my body. I don't dare get on the scale. I can't afford to have my day ruined.

Jake talks about my body like it is everything. I look down at stretch marks like flames running up either side of my stomach, breasts deflated now that I've had five babies, nursed three of them. Mirrors don't lie; they torture with truth. I look at the woman staring back at me. Why am I ashamed of my naked skin?

Looking in her eyes, I try to get her attention as she puts her hands around her waist to see if she can touch her fingers together. This is the daily test as to whether I'm thin enough.

I am fat. How can three words eat me alive? I stand there long enough to get a grip so I don't crumble onto the bathroom floor. I know what to do. I know what Jake likes me to do. Look good and be quiet.

He tells me he loves me the way I am, but I see him scope out women at church, at work, even in my family. It doesn't help when the kids tell me they see him looking too. When his hands touch me, I recoil. Is he feeling my fat?

I think about eating as often as I wonder if my gut is right. It tells me he's cheating. I search for something to numb the shame. I am fatally wounded, inherently broken. I am weak and nobody will stay. Nobody will love me forever. I just want to be beautiful to someone, someone's everything. I want to be a partner running into life to help fix broken people, broken families. People like me, families like ours. But I can't. And nothing I do can fix me or stop the chaos and pain that has hounded me from the day I was born. I can't stop the words that beat louder than my heart. *You're to blame. It's your fault. If you'd just get yourself together . . .*

I have to pick one battle. I don't know what's coming at me next. But if I can keep something under control, then I can keep pushing through. I try to keep Jake from looking at other women. If he leaves, I'll go through withdrawals. I've become addicted to him, how sometimes he tells me I'm good enough, or sexy, or hot, even if he never says I'm pretty. I know women don't stay hot forever. Then what am I going to do? What will he do?

What if I start with letting God look under the under? What if I let him push to the wound?

Men cheat on you when you can't give them enough, and then they blame you for it. I blame me for it.

That is heavy, little one. How are you carrying that through your days? Papa tries to break through my inner dialogue.

Food makes me feel better. Eating becomes tied to every emotion. I eat when I'm happy, sad, anxious, alone. It doesn't matter. I work hard to control my emotions with food, but it doesn't work.

Pandemonium is the house where my emotions live. But fullness sedates, keeps my emotions at arm's length long enough to muscle through the day. I want to eat more than starve. Laxatives help me do both. I'm abusing my body as my husband does, just in another way.

Papa tries again.

Food has become a god, little one, replacing much of what I want to do in you and for you.

Jake tells me I am perfect the way I am, that he loves my body. He pulls me close but never just to hold me. Hugging me arouses him. If I say no, he tells me I don't love him. All I want is to be held without strings attached. Held not as an object, but as a real girl. When I don't perform like a good object should, he tells me I have grandma legs, and he looks at other women. When I catch him looking at other women, when I see him undressing them in his imagination, he tells me what I need to hear: I'm sorry. I miss you.

I remember finding a picture on his phone, a girl he went to school with. He said it was no big deal. It was nothing. We were separated at the time. He says one thing. Does another.

I don't listen to his apologies anymore. I've become numb to those too. They happen again and again.

I don't leave because the cycle continues, and he cries and promises that we'll have a home: a family and a marriage that doesn't break, a man who stays, kids who love us, a church we attend together. This has been my dream since I was a little girl, and he knows this. He reminds me over and over again.

"I gave it all to you." he says. "I'm keeping my part," he says. I know he's lying, so why can't I just leave?

In church he even embarrasses us by wailing as he walks down the aisle. He lays prostrate on the floor in front of the pastor. He says he's repenting, that he wants to get saved. Again. Now we are trapped. The kids and I sit here turning blue, his performance sucking the air right out of the sanctuary. Sanctuaries aren't safe either.

Jake bars all my exits. My skin traps me.

I know God hears the dialogue I'm having with myself. I don't care. I need help. *Come down and disrupt the stage we're playing on.*

You are familiar with your brokenness. It is what comforted you when you were a baby. You pulled it close like a warm blanket. You stroked it to soothe yourself to sleep. You grew up no longer using a blanket. But you picked up the signals that marked you as an infant: Disappointment. Shameful. Broken. Helpless. Powerless. Little. Unwanted. Small. Voiceless. Lost. Unseen. Unknowable. No-name. Weak. Chronic. Awkward. Crazy.

This has been your mirror. You reflect the image bestowed upon you. Together, we will run my words back to the origin of the lie. I will touch it with gospel-medicine, then together we can practice new thoughts, new words in its place until one day, over time, the old image will stay dead and a new one will live, flourish even. One thought, one attitude, one habit at a time.

Let me reflect my image on you. Let me rename you. Let me retell you your story, who you really are. You'll know it's true because my words make the songbird in you sing. You are just scared it's too good to be true.

Little one, let me sing to you as I tuck you under the shadow of my wing.

Keep eating on my words. Don't starve yourself. Let me feed you. Let me call you daughter. Let me call you beautiful. I have gone ahead of you, preparing people and a place to mend you. Something like a heart-hospital.

I am making your way out. You are dropping breadcrumbs for your children and don't even know it. Someday you will drop bread-crumbs for others. You will be able to warn and help because you've gone through and come out on the other side. Keep moving forward, one yes at a time. That's how a lifetime of obedience is made.

Keep moving forward, one yes at a time. That's how a lifetime of obedience is made.

—Papa

chapter

twenty-eight

Order of Protection

The pastor, his wife, and their two sons eat dinner with me and my kids at our favorite Mexican hangout. We come here most Wednesdays and Sundays after church. This time is different. Jake isn't here with us. I asked him to leave the house because of the fight with Chelsee, my twelve-year-old daughter.

Jake had brought home Chinese takeout and set up a romantic dinner in the bedroom for us. He shut the door, locked it, then got upset when Chelsee pitched a fit because she didn't want him to keep the door shut and locked. She knocked on the door. Knocked again. Knocked again. That's when he lit up.

They began arguing through the door, then Chelsee began pushing in. Chelsee told him I didn't want to be in the room with him, and the arguing escalated from there. Fear and anger filled the room so I couldn't breathe.

The truth is, when it is just Jake and me, we are good. I think. Jake sees the kids as only bits to show in billfold pictures or to talk about in newspaper articles or to use to prove that we are "the fam" in church. They are only trophies to him.

When he went after Chelsee, it jolted me out of a fog, pushing me over the edge. I tried yelling over the both of them as he pushed the door shut and she pushed back, trying to hold it open. Chelsee called 9-1-1. I couldn't believe this was happening. I looked at the food he had set out. He went to great lengths; I felt sorry for him. At the same time, I'm scared of him. I didn't want to be in the room. I wanted to be out there with my kids. My room has become a battlefield; so has my mind.

The police came, and I was embarrassed, again. The neighborhood came outside to watch. The police told me the only way they could keep him out was with an order of protection. I called Brother Tim and his wife, Pam, and they took us to their house. I smelled it. The bread. She made homemade chicken and noodles and bread. Fed the kids and me. And there it was. The remembering. Grandma cooking for me when I wanted to stay with her instead of going back to Dad and my stepmom's. Ronnie making me a last supper from the last bit in our cabinet.

My nervous system is broken, and I felt as though I was on the edge of a breakdown, so we stayed there for the night. Grace, eight months old, slept in Pastor Tim and Pam's bedroom. Pam took care of Grace so I could rest.

Jake was angry, of course, and he came by their house. Tried talking to me. Tim went out, and Dakota tagged along to see his dad. Tim told Jake I wouldn't talk to him, and Jake was raging mad. He just about ran Dakota over when he peeled out of the driveway.

When I returned home, Jake wasn't there. Phillip, the pastor's oldest son, changed the locks. I didn't give Jake a key. He called the home phone a hundred times. He stood on our front porch, beating on the door for an hour at a time. I told him he's not welcome in the house if he's going to be so violent, so angry. His calling and stalking were incessant. Day and night. He beat on the basement windows. Tried getting in the doors. We covered the window with foil to keep him from looking in. Midnight had the kids and I in the hallway with our hands over our ears. The doorbell wouldn't stop ringing. Dakota couldn't stop crying.

I tell Pam I've decided to get an order of protection, an order by the judge, protecting me from Jake's temper, from his stalking, from his abuse. I wonder aloud whether the judge will believe me. I say I would have done it sooner, but I am petrified the judge will not believe me. As far as the community knows, Jake is too good. He is the husband every woman would want. Unless you live behind our closed doors.

Pam tells me she'll go with me.

Pam, her son Phillip, and Nikki go with me to court. I try and piece together what I'm going to say so that I make sense. I watch and hear other couples talking to the judge. Everyone can hear what is said. Then it's my turn. I look at Pam, and she nods her head for me to go, that I can do it. I go up and the judge asks me questions. I tell her the best I can. Then she asks Jake, and he gives her his story.

The judge asks what I need, and I tell her I need the newer Suburban for the kids. The old one has transmission problems, no air, and is rusted, but it's Jake's work truck. It isn't safe, Jake objects, saying he needs the newer one. He tells her it looks good for his customers. I want to defend myself, but I can't. I pray that she sees. She listens patiently, then answers him.

I can barely believe it. Did I hear her right?

She saw between the lines of Jake's words. She validates me, tells me I'm not crazy. I'm not wrong. I'm not seeing things. She says I can have the kids and the new Suburban.

I read Jake's body language, feel his energy. I look away and talk to Pam. But I feel him all the same. It is our turn. They take us into a room to sign more papers. A mediator explains the order of the court, and he cries like a little boy. His mad turns sad. My heart turns traitor on me. I feel so bad. He tells everyone he loves me and that he's sorry. Again, I cringe and shrink back, afraid they will buy his lies. Afraid I will buy them again. I have heard them so many times that I have them memorized. He pleads with me, and I sit there, wanting to run.

I love him. And I hate him. If I were two people, maybe I wouldn't have to choose, but I do today. I choose me.

The mediator gives me permission to go. I think I need permission. She senses that too. I think she wants me to know, though, that I don't need her permission, that I am my own woman.

Somehow, I begin to sense Papa telling me to stand, feel him pulling me up. I don't think I could do it otherwise. She tells Jake to stay there until we are gone.

Little one, nobody can upset my plans for you. Not even Jake. I'm not out there somewhere. I'm right here in your now.

Little one, I believe in you. See me leaning way, way over the balcony railing? I'm waving my hands over my head, yelling *above* the voices inside you. Let me help you. You *can* do it! Keep at it! Keep on! I'm right here; see me? That's right. I'm not sitting down. See me standing for you.

My heart is not a split-in-two heart. It isn't divided like people hearts. Like your heart. My unchanging heart is becoming your center, your wholeness, your unshakable foundation.

Remember, little one, my unchanging heart goes with you everywhere. Even in bedrooms, restaurants, and courtrooms.

chapter

twenty-nine

Idols

Since I said yes to God, I've been journaling my thoughts, my questions, and God's responses. But this morning, I sit at the table and read, you have "relied on oppression and depended on deceit" (Isa. 30:12). The words pull my face to them and say, "Sweet one, pay attention. You are shaping your life on lies."

I am? Am I putting all my trust in lies? This dream of a husband, a family, and a home? If it isn't real to Jake, then this dream I've put all my faith, energy, and heart into is a lie. Suddenly, I remember Satan is the Father of Lies. God only gives his grace, power, and strength for truth.

Is the dream I'm holding on to for dear life an idol? Have I been hungering for an idol all this time, thinking I was hungering for God?

I realize I'm trying to fix symptoms. Working from the outside in. Trusting God to get me out of things with Jake, and when he doesn't, I spin out of control. But God really wants to get my chaos out of me.

We are shaping our lives on lies. I'm shaping my life on lies! Oppression burdens my heart.

I've read stories in the Bible about battles and enemies, covenants and weapons, maps and ways of escape. About how Israel, in the book of Judges, lived in a cycle too. Just like me. They turned from God to idols. An idol is something you worship that isn't God. They believed in little gods or idols, did what was right in their own eyes, and began worshiping idols, believing the idols would save them. Then God would punish them, they would repent, then they would start worshiping false gods again. Their idol-worshiping ways held them captive. Helpless. They thought idols could protect them, deliver them. But the idols were the enemy.

Something wants this something-more in me. Am I sleeping with the enemy?

Reading through Exodus, I begin to see a pattern emerging that looks like veins beneath my skin. A map. A way of escape. How do I get out? How do I escape my idols? Show me what's next. Lead me out. For the first time I see that I am in a spiritual battle.

I turn to the story of Gideon, the Israelite and military leader on the brink of battling the enemy. God spoke to him, but he was scared, just like me. He questioned God. Just like me. He first tore down his family's altar to an idol, Baal, and built an altar to God. He was so scared that he did it at night, instead of the day. I read on. God took almost everyone away from Gideon before he defeated the Midianites. He slimmed an army of thousands down to three hundred men. God told Gideon to send the extra men home. God told Gideon to trust.

I feel a lot like Gideon, God.

Little one, I am looking for someone who will say yes. One who will take their destiny from my hands. One who will step up in their family to be the first. Who will go for me?

When I eat the words like breadcrumbs, chew them up, swallow them deep, they point my feet in the right direction. So many questions swirl in my life, yet this I know: these words will show me the way.

"Be my true north," I whisper. I can't tell what step to take next.

I sense him whisper, *read Abraham next.* So I begin.

You were not created to lie down for someone to walk all over you. Your back is not the ground. I am here to come alongside when life disrupts, dismantles, demolishes, disintegrates. I am the one to bring rescue through rewriting this story—let me.

I am going to shake you from the dust and lift you up and out. I have gone ahead of you, my love, and I have your back. I am on both sides. You are surrounded by me.

This dream isn't for you. It isn't for either of you. It needs to go. You are falling down before a man. You're praying to something that cannot save you. It is a lie. It doesn't exist. But I am your real.

Little one, see my gospel shattering the lie-bricks built up around your heart?

I want to rescue you and your children. My plan is not to hurt you and them, to make you stay in a place that destroys your family. I want to rebuild, repair, and restore. Once you're out, you can turn around and help others.

thirty

Experiencing God

M ost summer days are the same. The time of the court order has passed, and Jake is back. I struggle through his nighttime harassment—the hissing in my ear, his demands—but I wake in the morning and spend time reading, praying, listening for Papa, and journaling. The kids wake, eat, and we do our chores. We hang clothes on the line, tidy up the house, and prep dinner so we are done by 1:00 p.m. That's when the fun starts; that's when we walk three blocks to the pool. We splash, jump into the water, and play Marco Polo. We stay until four, then go home to get dinner on the table.

I feel the most at peace when I let the worry, weight, and wondering fall away and cook dinner for the kids, even for Jake. Something about the table centers me, even in so much uncertainty.

I've learned to love food again, to love feeding and filling my children. I love seeing people when they eat. Their faces relax, they smile, especially when we tell our God-stories around the table.

This is how I imagine my table. A generational table. Starting with me and my God-stories. It's my favorite place to drop bread-crumbs to my kids. They will inherit my table when I go home to heaven. They will inherit its stories, adding their own.

Cooking, baking, and eating around the table and sharing in this nourishment together is one of the most ancient things I know. I can't tell you why with any well-crafted sentence. But deep in my bones, I know extending biblical hospitality is more than mere entertainment. It is a safe place, a sacred place, and as much as I can, I will gather my family in it.

We are happiest when we eat off flimsy white paper plates, eating PB&J, off-brand potato chips, and Kool-Aid. But today I'm making my mom's homemade egg rolls. I savor the slowness of stir-ring pork, garlic, and onion, mixing cornstarch and water, wetting wonton wrappers. The kids come in asking to help. I move bowls, wrappers, and a tray over so they can join me. And we smile.

This. This is what my heart would give itself away to find. To keep. This is what people are starving for. What I'm starving for. I want to bottle it up right here—this belonging, this togetherness, this God-story in the making. Right now. I want to sit the kids down and tell them everything I know. For when I'm no longer here.

In my heart I know I must keep following the breadcrumbs, and I hope to show my children how to do the same. I'm learning that telling isn't enough. God is taking me somewhere, and my eyes are wide-open with wonder to discover where it all will lead.

It is a summer of contentment. I am home with the kids, home-schooling, going to the pool, to church. Jake has started his own construction business, so his days are full, and we are left more at peace than we have been in a long time.

I met a kindred friend a few weeks ago at the pool. She homeschools, loves God, and studies the Bible. She asked me if I would like to come to an Experiencing God Bible study with her. I agreed, and something inside me jumped. I told myself, *This is God! A friend, studying the Bible.*

This week as I do my lesson, I read that God initiates everything. I see for myself that God is always working. That I can join him. I don't find God. God finds me. My only job is to receive and follow. My heart says *this!* and jumps up and down. It tells me to pay attention. *The Experiencing God study is a breadcrumb, isn't it?*

My friend, she feels the same way. We can talk about our insides, God, and the Bible.

Experiencing God leads my friend and me to Precept upon Precept Bible studies, where we learn how to study the Bible for ourselves. I learn that the Bible is not a book of rules; it is a story. It has a once-upon-a-time. A beginning. And it has an ending. And everything in the middle is about restoration. Restoration of God's family. Restoration for my heart. For my kids' hearts. Maybe even Jake's.

I'm learning that I can string together passage after passage—even from different places in the Bible—like I'm stringing pearls. And when I do, when I see the dots connecting in this beautiful story, I get so excited that my heart bursts into flames.

My friend and I both have the same hunger to know God more. We take our kids with us. We eat our fill—at home, by ourselves, and in classes. We both end up taking classes to lead Precept. I want everyone to know God feeds us, rescues us, and restores us.

But this secret haunts me: my life is a wreck. I am desperate for restoration.

This morning, I am journaling all this, and as I take and eat the words, Papa speaks to me like a quiet whisper.

Little one, when you eat my words, when you live them in the middle of impossible, my words become like a handle that opens a door. A door that couldn't be opened for you any other way than through suffering—which made you look for breadcrumbs.

Follow me in the wilderness, my love. Follow my breadcrumbs. I'm leading you through a land of hard places, but you're not going alone. I am your Shepherd; you will lack nothing. I will lead you beside quiet waters. I am restoring your soul. All of this hard is our training ground. You are my warrior with a battle cry that only your voice can send out.

Will you let me into all the rooms in your heart? The kitchen too? I long to set a table for two. I long for you to join me there.

Little one, you can only truly lead through lands you've already experienced. There are some things I want to exchange in you. In these years I am going to lead you out of a church building into my wilderness. I am going to unhook you from everything. I will hem you in to awaken you to my ravishing love for you. I will show you what real true love is, what it feels like to be heart-naked and unashamed.

I take pain that is crumpling you and revise. Edit. I am always writing. Putting periods where there was a comma. Starting new sentences where there were run-ons. Taking rough drafts and making them smooth.

I am the author of the greatest love story ever written, the Bible. If you eat my breadcrumbs, taking me at my words because you have no other option, you and I will be writing the greatest love story ever told! This story will be yours! The one you dreamed of writing when you held the words written by your grandpa. You didn't know what it meant, but I did. I put everything you need for your sacred assignment, your greatest life adventure, inside your heart when I formed you, marked you, and breathed words into you. Words that live in you. Words that are taking you somewhere.

My words, taken and eaten, will pick you up, swing you around and around in my love. I will kiss you. Hug you. Pull you up on my lap and have long talks with you. Talks about everything—knowing who I am, what I'm like, and if my words can really be lived. Little one, they can. My Word will be enough to take you everywhere you go. Little by little. I work in your little, then multiply it. I write each story like each fingerprint—one of a kind.

When you look back over your years of wilderness, you will know me like you would not have known me any other way. Behind you will be breadcrumbs for others to follow. Sustenance. You will see what wasn't and be able to create with me to bring to life *not just something new* but something not ever seen before.

I am countering every move the
enemy makes to kill, steal,
AND DESTROY
you.
—Papa

chapter

thirty-one

Eleven Words

Chuck Lynch told us in counseling that healing begins with the parents, not the kids. I used to believe if my kids would straighten up and go along with what we wanted, things would get better. Chuck said it's needful to get to the lies and wounds, for it is only there that the gospel tears down and plants. This is only a work of Papa.

Jake and I are separated, again. He is going to a retreat called Grace Adventure, and I'm hoping this is the thing that turns him around. Turns everything around.

I'm out of options. Desperation picks up the phone and calls my dad, a man I don't know and who doesn't much like me. But I no longer care what anyone thinks.

These days pain monopolizes my attention, compromises my behavior, and clouds my thinking and maybe my decision-making too. But still, I need help. I know there are strings to help, but I don't care. I'm in pain and it's unbearable.

Dad meets me at McDonald's. I buy my own burger.

Awkwardness is a genetic trait. I got it from my dad. I look like him, and it strikes me that I know nothing about him. I want to ask him questions about his life. I want to ask him what he thought on the day I was born. I want to ask what he sees in my stepmom, why he listens to her and not me. But I don't say anything like that. I ramble about how the kids and I are having a hard time, and how, yes, I'm in church. As if church itself can save a life, save a family.

Dad tells me Jake called asking for thousands of dollars. No, I didn't know. No, I don't think he's on drugs.

Dad tells me it sounds like I'm in a wilderness season. He's been in those too. They are hard, he says.

I want help, Dad. Not a handout. I'm doing the best I can with what I know. I'm fighting to find a way out. I need help. Can you help me rent a house so the kids and I can have our own place and not be at Jake's mercy? But I don't say any of these things out loud.

My eyes look at his, and while he is talking, I know there is no help here. I feel it in his words as he finds his way around saying it.

I nurse a fantasy in that moment. Dad says things like let me help you. I know I wasn't there for you growing up. I'm sorry I wasn't, but I would like to be now. I would like to earn your trust over time if you will let me. No pressure. I want to get to know the woman that is my daughter.

And I fantasize my response too. Yes, Dad. Of course, I forgive you. I'm grown up now. I'm sorry too. You haven't seen all the pain that I've carried. I haven't seen your pain either. We've both been sitting on the sidelines.

But these are just fantasies. He says nothing like that.

Instead, he says, "Give your dad a hug. I love you, sugar."

That's it. *This is not what love is,* I think. But it is what love has felt like to me too often. An empty hug with no help. Hope you make it.

I walk outside. The sun squints my eyes, and I pull my hand up to block the light. Hot air blasts me in the face, blasting me with a dose of reality. The part that is born within every little girl and boy cries out inside of me. I want a daddy. Not a father figure. A functioning one. And for the life of me, I don't know how to find him. Loss leans me over the steering wheel, and I cry.

Papa's voice sounds through. *I am about to rebuild you. I am making life happen. My words are gathering you home. Whatever my words say happens. Not all at once, but they work until their job is done. Time is what you move through. My words are working right now. In this car even. Catch them. I didn't make you to fit in. I created you to stand out. Why do my children believe what culture tells them? It deceives. Everyone begins looking the same. Don't buy the lie that misfits do not belong. You are my misfit, and you belong to me.*

Papa, I take your words and eat.

I made you. I love you. I am pleased with you. Let this be your daily song.

I drive home singing my simple song. Eleven words. It is enough for today.

Let me lift your head, my love. Let me cup your face, touch your heart. Look into my eyes… my face is always in front of you. Never fading. Never withdrawing.

Little one, are you willing to believe the impossible? Are you?

I specialize in impossible stories. Trust me, I'm finding you in the midst of your pain. I'm setting a table for you. Here, in the missing of a daddy. Maybe he doesn't know your name, but I do. I know everything about you.

I'm teaching you to be awake to what I'm awake to. To see others' pain. Let me restore you to whole-heartedness, then you will enter into others' pain like a friend, a nurse, a pastor. You'll give a listening ear, a hug, a solution. Maybe even relief. You will live awake to others' pain, especially when their hearts ache for their missing daddy. You will carry the medicine, little one. Medicine that releases pain's pressure. Medicine that is gospel-medicine.

I knew you in your mother's womb. Before your lungs could breathe. Before your tongue could speak. I was your Papa then. I am your Papa now.

Don't buy the lie that misfits do not belong. You are my misfit, and you belong to me.

—Papa

chapter
thirty-two

Grace Adventure

After Jake returns from Grace Adventure, he seems changed, cured. It leaves me hopeful and wishing I could take him back in again. After all, he is so sorry. He tells me this again and again.

But insanity makes us do the same thing over and over again, expecting different results. Until you live through it and come out on the other side, you might not understand.

I don't understand.

I don't yet know trust is something that must be earned to be restored; it cannot be a slate wiped clean through a single apology. I have yet to learn that trust isn't forced. And I am still learning the critical need for a safety net of people for accountability. I know these truths in my head, but for too many layered reasons, the words and my heart haven't married yet. They aren't tools I can practice safely yet.

So much I don't know, but I'm following the breadcrumbs. Letting them lead me somewhere. Even if I don't know where, I trust them.

Little one, when you sit at my table, it's much more than a place to eat. It's a place of mutual trust and vulnerability. You are in a protected relationship with me. See? I am earning your trust, little one. You need to let me show you what real trust is. What trust looks like—trust from me and to me. You can't trust with a whole heart until you can live it. Knowing it is not the same as living it.

Little one, once upon a time, my children knew what biblical hospitality was. Who you eat with reveals something important about who you are, showing to whom you belong. My table means family and friends. You're my family; you're my friend. Eating at my table is vital; it is your survival. I want you to remember. I want to show you more.

I'm a father to the fatherless, little one. I want to protect you. I hear you crying out. I am setting your heart on a new foundation, my love. On a new course.

I am going to show up for you, just you watch me. I specialize in hearing words not said, in answering prayers that fear does not allow to be uttered aloud.

I haven't brought you here, my love, to kill you but to feed you. I will rain down bread daily. In just the right portion for you to chew and swallow. Enough for the day.

You are in need of rest and warmth. Let me hold you. Your heart is in extreme starvation mode. Let me give you small sips of living water, bits of bread. When you're stronger, you will come to my table to fill your ravenous hunger. I'll give you a meal prepared by me. From heart, to table. Here I will feed you a balanced meal. Exactly what your heart needs each day.

chapter

thirty-three

Conned

I am diagnosed with ulcerative colitis, an inflammatory bowel disease. The symptoms crept in silently for a long time, then dramatically, and now the disease is getting worse. The protocol isn't working. This time, I had a blood transfusion. I watched the nurses' concerned brows as they checked my vitals, uncertain. I was in that hospital bed for a week.

Shortly after getting home from the hospital, we move into our twelfth house on a bitter Christmas day. A day when most exchange gifts, we exchange addresses. We leave behind unpaid bills, set up our chaos someplace new as if it will be different this time. I will run a small home daycare program here. Nikki stays on to help me, since most days I'm too sick to do much. Chelsee and her husband, Phillip, open a donut and coffee shop a few towns over. Nikki and I coparent Dakota, thirteen, and Grace, nine. My health is precarious. My nervous system is tired. Tired from a lifetime of toxic relationships. All of us are.

Nikki helps take care of me when I can't. She is a watchdog over me and her siblings. I think she feels she needs to protect me. Maybe she does.

My quality of life has continued to spiral downward, but my pain tolerance is rising. I push through the days of in-home daycare from 6:00 a.m. to 6:00 p.m. Even with me working, after a year of struggling to catch up, we are still behind on rent payments and other bills. We are in an impossible cycle.

I am getting sicker, struggling through the days. I'm in so much pain. I have to take hot baths during the day, and I go to the bathroom 24/7—twenty-five plus times a day. I ignore the pain, muscle through for the money. It's my way to have something of my own, something I can control.

I'm panicking, afraid we can't make ends meet because Jake has been cheating his customers. Sometimes I find out we aren't getting a check at all. He tells me we are, but he's already used the money for another job. And he's taking money from other jobs to take care of our past due bills. It reminds me of the saying "robbing Peter to pay Paul." There is not enough money to catch us all the way up. He shuts one business down, and I tell him to put my name on the next one. I feel bad, but I think it will help.

It is so bad that a customer ran into us at Target last week, yelled at Jake, and told me I could do so much better than him. Jake is such a good liar that you believe him, the woman said.

Back at the house, I screamed at him, told him he's putting us in jeopardy. He told me he's not cheating his clients, and if I don't believe him, I can call his customers. He tells me this every time. I never do. Maybe I'm too scared to find out the truth.

I call his bluff this time. Maybe because I feel like I'm dying, and I don't care anymore. I call a customer when he is at work the next day. The customer tells me Jake has taken his deposit money but hasn't done any work. The man tells me of another client who has the same story. A story begins to unfold. Desperation hustles Jake to hustle folks for more deposits, but he never finishes the jobs. When he does work, it's shoddy work. He lies to everyone—me, the customers, maybe himself. And most of the customers are women.

One night, I call another customer, and the wife answers the phone. She tells me what's going on. He's told them stories, and they believed him. He's used me or the children as his excuses. He's thrown us under the bus, blaming my sickness, the kids' football and gymnastic expenses, whatever. He's said we're the reason he hasn't been able to stay on top of the work.

His customers sound like me, saying what I say. Victims of big promises and big lies. Maybe I'm not crazy. Maybe I'm just another customer, just another target for the con man.

The woman on the other end of the phone tells me there is no more money coming. They are finished with Jake. I hang up the phone so hard it could have shattered. I pull my truck into the garage, fearing it will be repossessed. Jake tells me we have a check coming. We don't.

The days tick by, and more and more customers come forward. The kids watch me rant like a lunatic as we discover he's cheated on family friends. He's even conned our insurance guy and the insurance guy's secretary.

Little one, let's string some pearls together. Remember the prodigal son and the running papa? The son who turned his back on his father, demanded his inheritance early, then squandered it? His actions were a mirror to his heart. His actions proclaimed that he wished his father was dead.

You once believed that saying the sinner's prayer, asking me into your heart, and getting saved was like going to the bank, cashing a check: you break the rules, Jesus pays the price, you escape punishment, and eventually go to heaven. As if heaven is all there is. Like I am just a police officer or a judge going around punishing sin.

Sometimes you still feel like that, yes? These statements are true, but there is so much more to the story. My story is how shockingly large my love is for my family. The story is about me, arms wide-open, welcoming the prodigals back to the family table. I want my family back.

I'm more than a ticket to heaven. I'm giving you a way back home, to me and my table, while you're still alive on earth. Your true belonging is at a table fellowship, with me. Letting me feed you bread and talk with you. There is room at my table. It is a table of grace, reconciliation, and restoration. It's time to sit down to dinner with me, little one. It will be the best meal you've ever had.

Soon, little one, you will see. You will know. I've been going before you, making a way where there is no way. Keep listening. Keep looking up at me. Keep following. You're going to make it.

chapter
thirty-four

I Tell Someone

Most mornings, I'm so ill that I can't get out of bed. Chelsee drives me to urgent care and they give me antibiotics and Valium. Ulcerative colitis is taking over. I've lost so much weight.

Back at home, Grace, now ten, is lying next to me, sick with a virus that has aggravated her asthma. Jake comes home from work and finds us both in our bed. I ask him to please make Grace something to eat. I'm too sick. He does and brings it to her, but he huffs and says she's in his spot next to me. He hates it when anyone threatens his place.

He comes over to my side of the bed and kneels down and asks how I am doing. He's sweet-talking and pretending to be all sincere, and I want to vomit. I feel the words crawl on my skin.

I want to say I feel like I'm going to die. He reaches his hand under the sheets and it creeps downward. I push his hand away. If I were a man, I'd punch him.

"I'm throbbing in pain," I tell him. I can't even think of what he wants. I can't wrap my mind around what he's thinking.

"You don't love me," he says. "You don't want to be with me. If you loved me, you would."

I no longer know which is worse: Jake or the chronic pain.

I lose it.

"Don't touch me! I'm dying, and you are living in a fantasy. I'm not your fantasy. I am real."

Chelsee calls my mom, and she comes over to check on me, asking if I want her to call the ambulance. I say yes. When I arrive at the hospital, the nurse asks me if I'm afraid at home, and for the first time I tell someone I am. I'm too sick to care anymore.

The hospital calls Hope House and they come late that night and ask me questions and talk with me. They tell Jake he can't come see me. The hospital protects me. I have Mom tell him to leave the house.

I have a blood transfusion, another colonoscopy, and IV steroids and pain meds. I'm too sick to help the kids. Dakota calls me and tells me he got in trouble at school. He is scared I'm going to die, he says, and then nobody will protect him. He will be left with his dad. I do my best to reassure him that I'm going to be okay and will be home soon enough.

I wonder when this will ever end, and I cry myself to sleep with the sounds of the hospital in the background. The whir of the machines. The rhythmic beeping in the hall. The drip of the IV. I feel powerlessness dripping into my veins like chemicals.

Ronnie comes up to care for the kids, and I've never been more grateful. He cooks tacos for the kids and stays with them. He brings Grace and Dakota up to see me. He is a good man, and he's never remarried. Grace walks in smiling, with a gift and flowers for me. Ronnie bought them for her to give me. When I hear this, I cry.

My child, I know—pain has become your chasm. Uncrossable. Eclipsing everything, within and without. Even me some days. You feel helpless, powerless, and alone in it. It may be uncrossable for humans, but not for Papa.

Remember, my love reaches across every uncrossable divide so we can walk together. No more alone. Ever. Now we can be together again. Father and daughter.

Keep trusting me when your feelings feel broken, when you feel you've lost your senses. Just take and eat; this is my gift.

It is in this place that I am finding you, my sweet one. Where you are taking, eating, and learning of me. Learning each beat of my heart, each beat pushing new life into you.

My love, I'm wallpapering my words to your heart. Pain is the glue. I am tearing down the old; we are building a house of belonging together.

thirty-five

Proof

My mom brings me home from the hospital after a week. I hope Ronnie is still at the house, but when I get there, he is already gone. I eat his leftover tacos and think, *I made a mistake. I got it all wrong. I am paying for everything. I am being punished.*

Since there is no check coming, I can't pay the rent. I am recovering in bed, so Mom comes and makes the hard calls for me—calls to the creditors and the landlord. The kids and I take care of each other, but they take care of me more than I take care of them.

All I can do is lie in bed. I can't sleep. There's too much on my mind. Steroids and vertigo keep me spinning. I am lost in my emotions, except today. Today is different.

Lying in bed, I look through our phone bills and see an unknown number. My gut tells me something is wrong. I call it and discover it is the number of a girl at the local bar. It's a friend of Jake's brother's wife. I ask a few questions, don't tell her who I am, and I find out Jake has been seeing her on the side.

Proof is staring back at me. I see it in numbers—dates and times.

What I've known in my gut has been right all along. But it doesn't feel like I thought it would.

I snoop a little more, find out that Jake has been at her house. With her children. Why should I stay? I keep believing God is going to do a miracle, and I know God can change a person. After all, isn't he changing me? But maybe I'm just using that as an excuse because I've been divorced before, and I don't want to go through that again. Even more likely though, maybe I'm staying because I'm afraid. Who will love me after they hear my story? How will I take care of the kids? How will I take care of me? How will I live sick? I have no safety net of friends to catch us.

For almost a decade I've trusted you to work a miracle in our marriage, Papa.

I stay because I don't know how to leave. How do I stop my heart from loving? I know how to love him, but I don't know how to love myself. I stand outside of my life and see devastation. But what about Jake? I don't see him being devastated.

I can't let life win. At all costs I keep going, keep taking and eating breadcrumbs. If I starve to death, who will take care of my kids? As the weight of life crushes me, I hold on with everything in me. I reach deep, grab the spine of the Bible, every word, every promise. I don't know how I'm going to make it through any of this. "Please help me, God," my only intelligible words. I dig out the gospel music in ancient stories and sing, even though I don't have my own words. Each step Jesus takes, I feel his bigness in the rhythm of the walking. I imagine him walking me through this hell. I'm holding on to the Word himself. That is all I can do most days.

I hear the tears that you believe nobody else hears. I've been wiping them since the day you were born. You've been in my hands. I'm standing outside the devastation with you. You know what I see? I see a little girl who wants to know she's not alone. She's safe. I see a warrior who looks different. You're my misfit who carries a sword in one hand and a crown in the other.

Little one, my arm is not too short that it cannot save. You are held. With the other arm I am fighting all of hell for you.

You are searching, listening. I was watching you when you were in your mother's womb, even though you didn't know it. You are no accident. No mistake. You were not born for the sake of suffering. Let me teach you to take up your sword of promises and swing it. I will show you how.

Let me teach
you to take up
your sword of
(promises) and
swing it. I will
show you how.

—Papa

thirty-six

Building Altars

I shuffle to the coffeepot and hit brew. It's still dark outside. Jake is away, working on a new railroad job. So I have some peace. The wood table is blemished and worn with years of life lived, crayon drawings, coffee cup rings. The table is my shelter in the midst of my story. Here I read my Bible, eat words alive, and build altars while the house sleeps. Coffee is my adrenaline. I light a single candle and sit down. I wrap my blanket around me, open my journal, and begin to scribble a prayer.

Monologue has turned into dialogue in my journals. As I stop wishing Jake will change—I know he won't, without a miracle—I turn to letting God change me. I spend more time looking up at God than at my mess. My Bible is laid open to Habakkuk 2:2–3 (MSG), to the words God gave me decades ago.

Full of Self, but Soul-Empty

And then God answered: "Write this.

Write what you see.

Write it out in big block letters
    so that it can be read on the run.
This vision-message is a witness
    pointing to what's coming.
It aches for the coming—it can hardly wait!
    And it doesn't lie.
If it seems slow in coming, wait.
    It's on its way. It will come right on time."

He reminds me of his promise as I sit. The words are like breath in my ear, causing goose bumps.

I close my eyes to see those words, imagining where they will take me if I believe them. Like steam slow dancing above my coffee cup, I hear, *I'm going to do something that you wouldn't believe even if I told you.*

Papa? You're telling me that even if you told me right now what it is you're going to do, I wouldn't believe you?

Yes, he says. *That is exactly what I'm saying. Write it down.*

I don't know what this means, Papa, but I write it down.

Memory traces back over my old journals, turns the pages of my history, searching for what I left behind, lost. I'm not sure what it is, but I remember when I first heard the music. When I was nine years old standing in front of the choir. Where I first heard God's voice. I was a nobody that God saw. Papa gently called me out of hiding. Like a romantic gentleman courting me.

Now he's leaving clues for me to find him again—breadcrumbs— and it keeps me reading more. Remembering takes my hand, nudges me forward. Today it's Habakkuk 2:2–3.

Papa, I don't know what the vision is, but today I don't need to know or understand. Oppression is devouring me in secret. Help me.

My love, believe me with your heart, not your eyes.

In my mind, I climb up on the table and lay down on rough wood, arms open on either side—forming a cross—and close my eyes. Somehow, I know God's vision is bigger than me and my story. It is tied to something other-than.

I want to be fully exposed in your light, Papa, filled beneath your fiery gaze. Look into me; do your work. Do it thoroughly. I know it is going to hurt, but I see the love in your eyes, Papa.

Papa tells me there is no anesthetic for this kind of surgery. Trust is the numbing cream. Gospel the medicine.

I know, I whisper, pulling my skin apart, exposing my naked heart to let him in. It's almost a relief letting him see it all.

I see words lying on my heart, sitting there a long time. Life's heaviness breaks my heart open, letting the words fall down into the cracks, through my skin, into the suffering places—the loss of one marriage (and looks like probably my marriage to Jake too), the loss of homes, the abuse, the body shame, the chronic disease that is now eating my life up like locusts.

Papa, it's deeper still.

He responds. *Yes, deeper. I only give grace for truth, not lies. Who is the Father of Lies, little one? I don't give grace for lies, for covering up. It is in the uncovering that I do my perfect healing to wholeness.*

I tell him what aches most is this gnawing angst in my own crushed spirit, my own inability, my own sin and selfishness. *My doubt, Papa. Not in you; in me. In my ability to keep moving forward. I want to blame everyone and everything else when it goes on and on like an endless nightmare that I can't wake up from. I know you see my innermost thoughts.*

I keep telling God, and now I say everything out loud instead of just writing it in my journal. I find it cathartic to give voice to my thoughts, to pound my fist on the table, to yell to the heavens, shaking my fist as I go down the list. "Oh, Papa . . . Help me. Help us. Come get us. Pick us up. . . . How are my kids ever going to believe this God I say I believe in? Who I take at his word. Show yourself big, God. Not only for me but for them. Come down, rend the heavens. . . . Do for us what you did back in the days of all the stories I read, God."

Words that never see the light of day fester, crawl around alive under my skin, having nowhere else to go, come out sideways.

"It's scary to say what lies deep inside my heart, Papa, but you are my safe place to say them. They aren't too much for you. I'm not too much for you.

"I bury my face in the Bible, inhaling your words, begging my senses to take me to some ancient time and place. If only I can touch the hem of your robe. I can't be close enough to you Papa, other than your words. It is the closest I can be to you as a person. I breathe in so deeply I swear I can smell your words releasing a thick woodsy aroma, like fresh cut cedar trees on a cold winter morning.

"Is this the fragrance that comes from worshiping and loving you, Papa? I beg for your love to set me on fire."

Papa's fire fills me, pulling my heart into an invitation to go somewhere. A story bigger than mine. One of creation and covenant. One that threads from Eden to Israel to Jesus to a new world in the making—a city Papa is building.

He says to remember this moment. *When it's dark, cold, and you can't see or sense me, remember. Remember what I have told you in the light. Remember me, to move forward. Look inside. Come back to this table. I'm always here, waiting. Remember: my story is going somewhere. We are headed home. Wait for the vision. Hold on to my promises with both hands when distractions come and tempt you. Wind them around your finger like a wedding ring. Following me is a circle, like a wedding ring. From life to death to new life again. It's an up and down pilgrimage. I am with you through it all.*

That's when I see it. I have believed the lie that Jake can do for me what only Papa can. I've made him god in my life. I've been demanding that he fix me, fix him, fix us. Just fix it so that I will be okay. A haunting pain, an unnamed pain, cracks, groans even, as truth comes like yesterday's rain—Jake can't fix this.

From then on, I see the table differently. Each morning, in my heart, I build an altar on this wood table. This is a table of hospitality where God fills and feeds me, but it is also an altar-table. I also must make an offering here, an offering of myself. I say yes to letting Papa remake me as I lay my dreams, hopes, and fears on this altar-table. I lay it all down, day by day, little by little, and try to trust.

I am the offering—my anguish, my despair, and my humanity. I offer it all, holding nothing back. I pull my morning time with Papa through my days. I tell myself there is an art to living courageously. And I'm saying yes to being discipled by it.

It is more than his words. It's Papa himself I want to know. To learn of him. To go where he goes. I know I am on a never-ending journey and that Papa is setting things in place if I keep saying yes and letting him.

I touch his words with my own hands, see them with my own eyes. I beg God to put his words into me. I clutch my Bible to my chest as if to will them in. *Papa, make your words alive inside me so I can live them.* I can almost feel Papa's smile, feel his love in the flickering flame of the candle.

All your pieces have been crying out to be found. To be made whole. I am taking out and putting in, kneading *shalom*, like yeast, into your heart. My bread is finding you in the pain, and you are eating it. You ache to be known. I am knowing you even now.

My love, come be with me. I only want to love you. I have no other motive. No hidden agenda. No strings. I've circled you with walls of cedar, marked you with my unmistakable fragrance. My family is known by their fragrance.

My love has marked you. You belong to me. Pain and persecution can never beat this fire out of you. It will only cause it to burn brighter. Endless floods will be unable to smother the raging fire that burns within you. I will stop at nothing as you surrender your all on the table, receiving my fire until one day it won't even seem like a sacrifice to you anymore.

It is on the altar you are beginning to receive my love, learning to live as my daughter, not an orphan. You have an ever-present help in your Papa.

My love never lets go, never abandons, cheats, or uses your heart against you. Ever!

Fasten me on your heart like a seal of fire, my love (Song 8:6).

I want to be your first love. I want your heart, little one. Always your heart. Will you trust me writing your story? Let the tracks take Jake on his own pilgrimage and you come with me for yours. I want to give you your inheritance. Will you trust me?

I only want to love you.

I have no other motive.

No hidden agenda.
No strings.

—Papa

thirty-seven

Railroad

Jake and I are separated yet again. I'm in a rental house across the street from my mom. He moved back to his mom's empty rental house.

Life has caught up with Jake and his businesses. Since he's working the railroad job now, he tells me he's seen the light. He's a changed man, he says. I spend too much time overthinking his answers, his whereabouts, and his intentions though. He cannot not lie. I doubt everything when I'm with him too long—my reality, my heart, even my existence. I'm exhausted from listening to his excuses, cleaning up his messes, trying to make a crooked line straight. This is an unfixable situation. Every fiber of my skin tries to protect me from the rawness of reality, the impossibility of it all.

Disappointment that God isn't going to save our marriage sets in like winter. I see no human way out. What kills me the most is the cycle of hope: tasting what it can be like when we are in our honeymoon phase, because when I pretend I am okay without a voice, it's very good; but when it's bad, it's awful. We are clenched teeth hiding behind smooth lips.

I know how to be what Jake wants me to be so that life will be smooth for six months. We live in a cycle. We move, start over. I have to play pretend. If I am what he wants, we are good. I know what he wants. I have become a parcel of property. After managing my chronic disease and his deceived customers, I have little energy to help the kids. They are being taken under too.

I exchange my name and my adventure for food, clothing, and shelter. Internal for external. During the day we talk about the weather and how his day went, and at night he forces sex on me. I keep house, cook dinner, and manage the lie called our life. Sick. Sickness and abuse have turned me into an accomplice, taking my kids hostage in this life with me. When he's gone, the kids and I talk about how we're trapped, how we will survive, and how we will get out.

Jake can't hear me living. Papa does. Jake has never felt this otherworld, incommunicable pull that woos my heart. I know that when I'm dying I will not have lived at all, and that terrifies me. Will I die without being unlocked to live into this thing I was made for? Will I die without learning how to live whole? Will I die in the shape of a question mark? Will I die in the shape of shame?

I am making plans in my journal to escape my marriage, maybe start a new life. An escape where I'm no longer dependent on Jake for money, love, and knowing. An escape where my heart doesn't depend on him to be okay. I don't know how any of this will look, but I'm listening in the early mornings at the table.

Jake comes to tell me goodbye. He lives the town over. Then I watch Jake drive away in my car, back to the railroad, gone for days. I watch him fade into the future and cry for everything that isn't and everything that could be, wondering aloud, "What's next, Papa?" Then I feel it. The wind.

The I-need-hims start playing in my head; the guttural cries of the orphan churn in my heart. I feel them as real as the wind on my face, but as I watch the wind blowing leaves, I sense Papa's breath blowing hope deep into the hollows of my heart. It's the voice of Papa. His voice, like a key, slides into the hollow of my heart. Click.

You have a choice, little one. You can go down the road you've always gone down, like an orphan who has no father to care for her, or you can let my words spoken to you like a handle pull you up inside this moment. Give me the hurt, the need-hims. Trust this railroad thing. Let me give you something you've not had before. More of me.

I hear him speaking, pulling me into his arms.

You are learning to eat my words. To chew them. Swallowing them deep down inside. Your heart absorbing the nutrients.

Little one, what do you want to be free from?

You don't know it yet, sweet one, but you have your own rebellious heart. You are actively resisting my rescue, my transforming grace, and all the consequences for the way you are living your life. Keep going. I'm showing you. Going with you.

You are aching to be free to be a daughter, not an orphan. My grace, little one, comes only in the discovery of your total helplessness. You are like a caterpillar in a ring of fire. Rescue can come only from above. Right now your eyes are on the fires coming at you, rather than me and my rescue from above.

You've lived like an orphan so long. But you are my daughter, and you belong at my table.

It is in eating my gospel-meal that you discover me as your Papa. You are my daughter. You are forever family. Still, I will show you your need to come daily to eat my words, to renew your relationship with me again and again and again. This is how rescue will come: daily, over a lifetime.

thirty-eight

Heart Map

This inflammatory bowel disease is eating away at my emotions, my insides, and my day-to-day living, creating only so many hours a day that I can function. I spend more and more time sitting on the toilet, whispering the same prayer: "I can't take one more thing, God. I can't take any more pain."

I sit on the toilet, thinking about Jake. I dissect the years of separating, coming back together. Where it went wrong. Or if it was never right.

Jake's unending harassment makes my fingers and toes clench, and when I give in, I clench everything so hard I will my bones to break. I imagine that my bones breaking will somehow feel good, better than enduring his bottomless need. Helplessness and power-lessness pulse through my body as he takes me. The whole time I scream in silent hate, imagining my brain might burst if he doesn't hurry up. Maybe that would send him a message. Maybe the scream isn't only about the moment. Maybe it holds all the pain of all the years I couldn't speak up for myself.

These are my thoughts as I sit on the toilet today. I pray for God to help me find my voice.

Finishing up in the bathroom, I head to my table where Papa reminds me he won't let go of me.

God, I will trust you. You are more than enough. Even in the pain, the blood, even with this wasting disease, this emotionally absent and abusive husband, these broken relationships, you are more than enough.

Everything is changing. My insides dizzy with discovery, I sit down, imagining myself in my very own house of belonging. I see a table in the center of this house, like an altar-table that's ever burning.

I read my starting-place words he gave me decades ago, Isaiah 58:9–12 (MSG). I read them again.

> If you get rid of unfair practices,
>> quit blaming victims,
>> quit gossiping about other people's sins,
> If you are generous with the hungry
>> and start giving yourselves to the down-and-out,
> Your lives will begin to glow in the darkness,
>> your shadowed lives will be bathed in sunlight.
> I will always show you where to go.
>> I'll give you a full life in the emptiest of places—
>> firm muscles, strong bones.
> You'll be like a well-watered garden,
>> a gurgling spring that never runs dry.
> You'll use the old rubble of past lives to build anew,
>> rebuild the foundations from out of your past.
> You'll be known as those who can fix anything,

restore old ruins, rebuild and renovate,
make the community livable again.

Read them until you embody them, my love. Let go of the trying to get it all right. Let me lead from inside you. These words are what the wilderness will do inside you—take out the empty places and fill them.

Old rubble . . . full life in the emptiest of places . . . rebuild . . . restore . . . renovate.

Papa, I love these words.

I go back to the beginning. Read it again. Ask the text questions. Who. What. When. Where. Why. And how.

I notice lots of ifs and thens. I circle them. I pay attention to the things I need to be doing if I want to see the promises come about—the "if" actions before the "then" promises.

I flip to Genesis, to the story of creation. I read it again, this story of the God who acts. I read all the verbs I'd circled in Genesis 1. I'm starting to understand! I'm seeing patterns in the ancientness of God's voice, in the context of each story. As I question the story, I'm in awe that it talks back.

When God uses his words, things change. When I act on God's words, things change.

My love, you see it, don't you? I open eyes to see through the temporary into the eternal.

This morning, the words of Genesis come alive, and I take and eat. The eating strengthens me. This story nourishes me. It makes me hungrier than ever. I find I think less about God rescuing me and more about where he is leading me. Something is shifting. I can't explain it. He is opening my eyes to see that he has a plan, maybe even an adventure.

I go back to reading.

God engaged with Abram and Abram responded. God helped Abram by doing the heavy lifting. God gave promises; he vowed, "I will." God asked Abram to go on a journey with him.

Daughter, I want to do your heavy lifting. Will you let me show you? It isn't a quick fix. It isn't a cliché new beginning. It is a lifelong follow-through. But I will travel with you. Through storms, waves, and rain, I've never lost the way.

I read on. Abram responded and received. What did he receive? A life-map charted for him, to his own land, to a home for generations upon generations. God's words are a map.

I have longed for a wild adventure, something bigger than my present reality. A promised land for me and my family. And here it is! An invitation to pioneer a new land.

Let's do it, little one! You are wandering, but I can lead you out.

Is this a map to my escape? I have traveling to do with you don't I, Papa? You've been speaking this to me all along. You want to lead me somewhere, don't you?

Yes, my love. You're hearing my voice.

It isn't over yet, is it?

No, my love, it is going to get harder. But remember, I am with you every step of the way. You are letting me make a way for you and for your children, grandchildren, and beyond. You are your family forerunner.

I start drawing a map of my heart in my journal, like the ones in my Bible. My entry starts with the beginning. The cross. The door. I mark the places I've been, the altars I've built, the giants I've fought, the ones I'm fighting, the forks in the road, the mountains and valleys, the shadows. Then I draw a compass.

As I draw, Papa leads me to Deuteronomy 8:2–3 (MSG).

Keep and live out the entire commandment that I'm commanding you today so that you'll live and prosper and enter and own the land that God promised to your ancestors. Remember every road that God led you on for those forty years in the wilderness, pushing you to your limits, testing you so that he would know what you were made of, whether you would keep his commandments or not. He put you through hard times. He made you go hungry. Then he fed you with manna, something neither you nor your parents knew anything about, so you would learn that men and women don't live by bread only; we live by every word that comes from God's mouth. Your clothes didn't wear out and your feet didn't blister those forty years. You learned deep in your heart that God disciplines you in the same ways a father disciplines his child.

Dear daughter, my calling is not out there somewhere, it's cradled within you. You've been following the homing instinct like a tiny bird inside you, here, to this moment. A calling that is a belonging. It is my gift to you. It is personal. Immediate. And real. If you follow the name I gave you and leave everything from the name you were born into, I will show you a new home-country. I will create within you a house of belonging. I will remake you, rename you. I will bless you and your family line after you.

Read my words until you embody them, my love. Let go of the trying to get it all right. Let me lead from inside you. Let me be your compass from here.

chapter

thirty-nine

House of Belonging

One morning when I am at the kitchen table writing, Nikki comes in and asks if I have ever thought about starting a blog. I've heard of them but never read them.

I'm following adoption blogs, she says. She has wanted to adopt since she was twelve.

"Mom, you're always processing out loud to us kids. Why not start a blog?"

And a seed of possibility is planted.

When I read Bible stories about people that had hard lives, it's like mining darkness and digging out gold. Stories help me remember that I'm not alone. Maybe if I take the journaling of my heart, all of its pain and laments, and put it on a blog, I'll find others traveling the same road.

I get up the next day and start a blog. But what should I name it? I want it to be a bone-deep name. One morning, while sitting at the table, it comes like the snap of a finger.

House of Belonging.

It's perfect. Don't I remember reading those words somewhere when I was younger?

I always anticipated our community-wide annual garage sale. I was able to save money buying the kids used clothes. I always came away with a truckload of finds: clothes for the kids, gently used toys, and pretty things for the house. And books.

My eyes rummaged through tubs of books when a title caught my eye. *House of Belonging.* I literally dropped my stuff to pull it out. Instantaneously, blood rushed to my heart. As quickly as I had pulled it out, I put it down. Dakota and Grace were arguing over army men and a Barbie house.

I can't sleep. House of Belonging keeps me up. Not even the sound of our box fan lulls me to sleep. It's like there is a blank page begging me to write, something invisible begging to be visible. I can't figure out why those words move me. But they do.

House of Belonging—it feels like a fairy tale, a faraway dream, yet as close as my skin, holding all of my memory.

A house of belonging—it's what I've always wanted, really.

And though my internal home is full of places that hurt, I can let Papa create a House of Belonging within me. If I let Papa give my heart his shape, then I can share it with others. If I let Papa design my life on a cross, maybe I can live into the shape of Jesus. Jesus isn't a dream but a way to follow. In my House of Belonging, there is a long table. Papa tells me I have a place there. If I pull up a chair, he will feed me.

Jake and I are living together, but separate. I can't afford to live by myself with the kids. I need his money to live. We agree that he will live downstairs and I will stay in our bedroom. We still love each other. We still tell each other. Neither of us know how to fix it. Fix us.

Nikki tells me about the Nester, a blogger who decorated her rental house on a budget. I click through her blog, and I'm inspired. Nikki and I will go to flea markets and find good used furniture. We'll decorate our front porch for fall, decoupage our kitchen table, and do a few DIY projects. And we'll blog it all.

The plan is good, but my heart is ever reaching for the deeper things of life. I need heart-words. God's words are my soul-medicine.

I don't know how to merge the two—home decor and heart. Could I create some sort of art with words—words that have given such life to me? Something people would want to hang in their homes? Could I sell it on my blog?

Once, when I was married to Ronnie, I made wreaths from fabric scraps. My mother-in-law sold them at her work; she sold a lot of them. She told me I was creative. I had never been told I was creative before or since.

I read once that God doesn't get the address wrong. In all the moving, I've learned it's true. I see now how Papa has given me breadcrumbs, like gifts.

This time is no different. This gift is a person. Her name is Lisa. We live across the street from each other. She is married to a veterinarian. They have four children, one adopted. Her oldests, a twin boy and girl, are Grace's age. Once they get past their shyness, they become fast friends. So do Lisa and I. We go deep, quick. Our friendship grew over the summer: swimming, long morning walks, and heart-to-hearts over coffee.

Unintentionally, our walking became holy ground. I slowly opened up a little about what was happening at home. More importantly, in my heart.

In our walking something found us: her next adoption and my business. But neither of us knew that yet. We keep walking and talking it out most mornings.

This particular morning, I lace up my shoes, put my hair in a headband, down a coffee, waiting to eat until I am done walking.

Lisa is a good listener. She lets me process out loud about how I need to make money to get a house on my own. She knows I can't work outside the home because I am sick. She brainstorms ideas with me.

One time, I saved money and applied for an apartment. Lisa knew the property manager. She thought that would help me get in. It didn't. My credit is bad, they told me. And I had no job. They said no.

No would have spiraled me down a year ago. Feelings of being alone, not having enough money, and feeling trapped would have had me looking to Jake to make me feel better. Ever so slowly I'm learning that that is false. If I choose to obey God's words, I can resist the enemy's games. I take his words and hold on to them in the hard that I am in—standing instead of crumbling.

Then I remember! I tell her about the wreaths I made for

Ronnie's mom, and she asks if I have ever heard of Etsy. I haven't. She explains it all, encouraging me to start a shop. Maybe you can make wreaths again, she says. It is a good idea. Maybe I could make wreaths using coffee filters, dyed with tea, stamped with words: tea-stained coffee filter wreaths.

More weeks pass, and my pain flares up. Between doctors' visits and a stint in the hospital, Nikki and I work. We tell Jake only what he needs to know. There's no reason to test his anger, his mechanisms of control. I had been in remission from ulcerative colitis. I had been on Remicade for six months. I had gotten state Medicaid.

But now my ulcerative colitis is worsening. Pain debilitates my daily life. Here I am back where I started. Nothing is working so Dr. V, my GI, has to figure out what to do with me. I'm getting worse. Just like our abusive marriage cycle.

Nikki and I open House of Belonging on Etsy, selling wreaths with words. We sell just enough wreaths to break even. The income is nice, and it encourages me to teach myself how to sew. We try to think of other things we could put in the shop, things to make a profit. I buy a cheap sewing machine and create patterns for applique owl kids' T-shirts and hats. I share them on the blog, and they begin selling too. It is only a little, but it encourages us.

I see Papa's provision, even in the pain.

In the chaos, I'm practicing seeing with my heart. Sometimes I see Jake in ways I haven't before. I sometimes see past his dysfunctional behavior, emotional upheaval, and lies and distortions . . . into his wounds. Into his little boy. I ask Papa to give me his eyes to see others like he does. In his faithfulness he does. I don't want my heart to grow hard. I want to be safe and free, not hard. It is difficult to see into another and yet not be able to fix. I also see how my behavior, distortions, and emotional upheaval cause him to react. We both need rescue.

What began as a way to make money now uncovers a childhood memory: my grandpa's legal pads—stories with unwritten endings—and holding history in my hands. Something living between the dead.

You're alive, little one.

Blogging is connecting me to my something-more.

What encourages me more is the blogging community of women who love God's words like I do. I write posts about what God is doing in our lives. We are telling our God-stories and in a small way, it's giving my life handle bars to hold on to. I think I'm finding women who sound like me! A light is beginning to shine inside the darkness from the outside.

I begin wondering what it would be like if I had this in real life. People who know my real name, who see my gifts. People who don't try and squeeze me into something I'm not. What would that look like? I don't know, but I want to try.

While I spend my days dealing with disease and Jake, I'm choosing to practice the words Papa feeds me at the table. I'm spending more time looking at God instead of my mess. I'm finding out through blogging that most people don't know what the Bible says for themselves because they don't know how to study it with their heart. I encourage them that I was the same before God brought the Experiencing God Bible studies into my life.

I spend most of my time choosing to let go of old habits, patterns, routines, and issues, deep diving into what has been holding me back. I'm making space for new. I'm intentionally choosing joy each day too. Even when I don't feel it; especially when I don't feel it.

I tell the kids my God-stories every chance I get. They still roll their eyes, telling me my mind goes into microscopic mode. I automatically zoom in to everything that is happening. And I don't keep it inside. I talk my thoughts out loud. Right in the moment, says Grace.

Grace tells me I turn everything into an inspirational quote.

The oldest three are grown now. Even still. I tell them. It's my favorite thing in the world: to tell and listen to God-stories told around the table. A table set with the best meal I've ever had.

Little one, your desire for our sacred adventure is growing. Our story is headed somewhere. You are turning from things that leave you empty to my words that fill you and leave you hungrier than ever. Choosing to let me feed you isn't hurtful in the same way eating emptiness is. You are discovering this, yes? You are my favorite, little one. Look at you! You were made for me. For Papa. I smile every time I look at you. You are a fighter. I made you a fighter. Now you are letting me have the fighter in you, to grow her up. You were made for this pilgrimage, little one. Oh, in case you ever wonder, you do know what to do. And when you forget, go back over the words that I have spoken to you. Remember the words I spoke to you in the light.

A choice is coming ahead. A fork where you will have to take me at my word because you will have no other option. You must be willing to let go of what is comfortable, safe, familiar, and predictable so you can take hold of what I'm going to give you. Be willing to say no to many things to say yes to me.

chapter

forty

Words Matter

L isa takes me to places I have never been before. Stores with beautiful things. Stores I can't afford. Such stores used to make me jealous, wishing I could have any life other than mine, but now I go with gratitude and for inspiration. I'm learning that friendship is helping carry one another's weight, helping them do what they can't do for themselves.

Today, she takes me into a home decor shop in the center of an old historical town in Independence, Missouri. She wants to show me a sign she saw a few weeks ago. She said it reminds her of me. I've never put decorating my house at the top of the list, mainly because I couldn't afford it. But today, dots begin connecting as she points out the sign to me, asking if I've ever seen word art like that.

I haven't, I tell her. It is beautiful.

Looking at it I begin envisioning family, words, and food, and how these things bring us together. I begin to see how words like on this sign can be a banner over us. Maybe they can even make us a living sign if we eat living words.

I'm like a kid in a candy store. I can't wait to process this with Nikki. I'm wondering if we could make something similar, only with living words. Words about Papa, pain, and overcoming. Words that put land under families' feet. Words that give women handles to hold on to. Words that give men reminders that they are strong and full of courage. Words that remind us there is a story we belong in and that there is a Storyteller. That he is writing our story with his love. Words that remind us that he gave Jesus so he can have his family back, us back. Words that turn our homes into lighthouses, leading everyone safely home. Could we create pieces that share what Papa is like?

Lisa's birthday is coming up, and I want to give her a sign for encouraging me to write, to open an Etsy shop. Jake is still living in the bedroom in the basement, and he has all the tools we need to make the sign. I don't have to buy anything. I ask him to teach me how to use the chop saw, air nail gun, and tape measure. I am terrified of the saw! I have never used tools, let alone power tools, in my life. I might be out of my ever-loving mind. But that's okay. I go heartfirst, all in.

I failed math in high school, so the measuring is hard, and I made lots of mistakes. My mind doesn't work mathematically. I am books, writing, and daydreaming, not hammer, nails, and wood, but I keep saying yes even though I am slow and afraid. Jake teaches me how to cut a board and frame it and what materials would be best. I hand paint the letters using a projector. It is tedious tracing this many letters with pencil, then going back over them, painting them in, but in the end, the sign is beautiful, if I do say so myself.

Lisa loves her sign. She hangs it above her fireplace. I love how it makes me feel; seeing her hope in her words makes my hope bigger. My hope is that those words make a way for her to find her something-more. Her mom sees the sign when she comes over to visit and asks if I can make some for her flea market booth.

That's how it all started: morning walks, telling our God-stories. It started where good things always do: with words that matter.

Nikki designs and I build a few signs. We put them in the shop. We work around my sickness, her job, and the heavy darkness of chronic abuse and trauma.

We build everything on a foundation of chaos. I am in no frame of mind to think clearly. The only thing I manage to frame are signs. The pain wracks my body, and I go back to the hospital. They put me on steroids, give me infusions.

Even though I'm sick, even though there's so much chaos, Papa encourages me. And not just by my growing business either. He reminds me to remember back over my story, how he has brought me this far. He hasn't failed me. He won't fail me now.

God's words are my daily food. I pull up a chair every single day and let him feed me. I don't have a choice. Not really.

I ask him to reveal more of himself to me. I read about Abraham, Moses, Jeremiah, and Job. Everyone really. I see people just like me: ordinary people who found themselves in big messes. I observe how they believed God and took him at his word without seeing where they were going. Just like me. How they had nothing left to lose. Just like me. My family thinks I'm weak and needy. My own family is wreckage. My inside is wreckage, but I sense Papa's hand in my life, in my business.

I'm learning that when life lurches, I can turn in, to the center of my heart, to the table where Papa has prepared a feast for me. I let him feed me. And even if life is still careening, my heart isn't going with it. Not anymore; not since I've found this center. Whatever happens, I just keep coming back to the table.

I once thought rescue was a single event. Now I see it is a daily rescue. A daily coming to the table, letting him feed me gospel. Every single day. It's beautiful. Simple. It's enough.

I somehow know my story won't have a pretty bow at the end. Papa tells me he has that taken care of. To trust him. Each day is a new opportunity to say yes. I've never been a bow kinda girl anyway.

I'm starting to feel the ground beneath my feet, this land God has given to me and to my family.

I have a business. Where'd that come from? I laugh about it, sitting at the table this morning. And now, I'm secretly saving up money to get an apartment on my own, to get out of this abuse. I want to make a house of belonging in real life, a place of my own.

My love, I love the fire in your heart to take me at my words. Little by little, you are letting me dismantle your kingdom and rebuild with mine, setting your heart on a stable foundation, making it your own house of belonging. The house is what's inside. Where I live. A sanctuary. We are framing walls and windows and raising a roof. My words and your heart's yes are the raw material.

My words are visual reminders, signs framing your life. I feed you my words. You become a touchable, visible story. I embody hearts, making them a sign, a living story. Your life will be my heart-house. Inside you—a place to belong. Together we set up house. I am your bridegroom; you're my bride.

chapter

forty-one

When the Compass Moves

W e're a year into blogging, sewing, and making signs. Four
months ago, we moved from the previous rental where
I slept upstairs, Jake downstairs, and into separate houses. Jake
cosigned a lease for me on a house across the street from my mom,
and he moved into his mom's now vacant house a town over, where
he grew up. His mom had purchased land in the country, set herself
up to retire.

"I'm not moving to that old house," was the first thing I
told Papa.

But the more Nikki and I talk, the more we think it might work.
It is bigger. We'd have a basement to make signs and bedrooms for
each one of us. We could paint, pull up carpet, and maybe one day
remodel the moldy bathroom.

After talking it over with Jake on the phone, he agrees. A couple
months later, Nikki, Dakota, Grace, and I move our belongings to

Dakota and Grace's Nana's house in my yellow Ford pickup truck. It takes more loads than I can count. I'm exhausted, overwhelmed, and a bit excited. We are moved in.

Though it is the last place I wanted to move, I know this is what Papa wanted me to do. It is a broken-down, battered old house full of remains—memories with nowhere to go—but it has a basement we can work out of, and Nikki and I set out to make good use of it.

The basement is dingy and has very little room to work and little light. We carve out a space in the shape of an L among the boxes, tools, and unused furniture. We paint and frame on the cold concrete floor. I stain sticks and frame signs in between a workbench and a washer and dryer. The basement has flooded twice with sewer water. It is old, damp, and full of cobwebs, but it is enough.

For two years Papa is keeping us here in tangible ways. I call it my in-between place. In this house, my health hits rock bottom. The walls of this house hold memories of Jake's childhood—painful memories and good ones too. The walls hold generational sins and blessings.

Even in its disrepair, the kids and I fix it up the best we can. Paint covers most anything. We do a lot of painting.

This is the house where God's words become visceral and right now. Where God is becoming more real than he ever has been. Where I become real too.

Nikki and I close the business the last three months of the year because my hospital stays put us behind on orders. It is still just the two of us. I stain, paint, trace, frame, and box the signs. Nikki designs them around her nine-to-five insurance job. She pitches in with me when she can.

During the closure, I'm in bed when I'm not working down-stairs. Sickness forces me to bed. To be still. By God's grace I see it as an opportunity to let him take me somewhere, show me some-thing more of him. I listen, talk, and cry often. I don't have words to put on the pain, but he doesn't seem to mind. He is showing me beautiful treasures in the darkness.

Jake comes home for a week at a time. He is gone six to eight weeks and then home a week. So ours is a slow separating. The weeks in-between his coming home, I begin to have space to breathe. Space that lets God uncover the real me.

Last time Jake was here, we asked him to build us a wall for an outside photo shoot. He did. Nikki and I put book pages on it. I wonder if people have forgotten. If they will see the beauty of the words or not.

We reopen shop on January 1 with a brand-new collection of hand-lettered signs called Deeper Still. The name of the signs came from my time with Papa. Even though I was in tremendous inner and outer pain, I asked him to go deeper still, into my heart. There was more work I knew he wanted and I needed him to do. Sales of the signs blow up. I can't sit at the table much. I am too sick. My bed is my table.

Sitting in bed this morning, writing it all out to Papa, I take and eat a gospel breadcrumb. I know he is inviting me to write with him. He is asking for my once-and-for-all yes to writing my story with him. I give him my pen and paper, my blood and heart. And I say yes to whatever story he is going to write next.

I think it is the rebel in me that has always led me down hard roads, and even though this road is still hard, it's a different road.

Little one, dream with me.

It's as if I'm his greatest love, and he wants to give me everything my heart desires.

I'm thankful for how God has helped the kids and I so far. Thankful for where we are today. Thankful for the tomorrows too. I know his hand is on me, the kids, and the business. I say out loud, "No matter what, I'm not giving up, Papa." And I mean it.

It feels like I continually fall on my face, Papa. I'm holding on to you and your words.

I have a sense deep in my bones that something is changing. Again. I can't explain it.

I spend time reflecting over my journals, rereading what God has done. These are words he has given me, my family, maybe even the world. I listen more, write more. I'm waiting and watching for when I am to do something, when I am to join him. When the compass moves, so will I.

The next week a house for rent in the town over finds me. Could this be my first house all by myself? With only my name on the lease? It is a breadcrumb. I take and eat.

You are the one changing, love. Situations and circumstances are chaotic, but they are changing your heart, see?

You are following the signs, going deeper still. You're picking up the breadcrumbs, eating them.

I know it's hard and there are obstacles, but I'm making a way through. And I'm going through with you. You will see it soon. I am turning things right side up. I am fighting for you and nothing or no one can stop me. I am unstoppable. Always working for you.

See yourself as bigger because I'm bigger. Rest on what I can do.

Soon, my fiery warrior, we will be dancing on the mountaintops. Together we are unshakable. Keep stepping up on my words. They lead you up and out.

Home is the destination. Everything else is only a station on the way.

Daughter, remember the words I've given you. Keep them always in front of you. Set your heart on them. Write them out. Sound them like a ram's horn, a battle cry of freedom, arousing my messengers. Proclaim my gospel of put back togetherness. Daughter, proclaim freedom all over the land—for you, for others. It's your birthright.

forty-two

I've Been Named

My disease keeps me cramping, straining, swelling. I live in ache. I have accidents in restaurants and flea markets and when I try to run to the Target bathroom. I always scope out the bathroom when I walk into a store. I live in chronic embarrassment. I have tried everything.

I lay down and close my eyes. Papa keeps me company in my misery.

When I close my eyes, you're still the only one I want to hold me. You're the only one on my mind, Papa.

I tell Papa I wish I had people I could talk to. People that would listen with their hearts. People that wouldn't be scared of the pain but would hunker down in it with me, tell me God-stories, remind me I'm not alone. They might not know what to do, but they would stay. Be here. Be people who help, not hurt.

I've become a fossil. Dead. Pressed into mud. Evidence from an earlier period. Formed by minerals in the earth's amniotic water, my bones and tissue create a replica in stone of the original me.

I do not pretend to love you, making demands on you to perform or else. I do not love you to control you. That is not love.
—Papa

This home is fragmentary, petrified, and primitive. I wait to be taken to my true home.

I wake up in Papa's arms, and I go to sleep in them. Each day fades into the next, and I despair that I will never be in the land of the living again. I watch it from my bed like a black and white movie. I'm an unseen spectator, an inconvenience, as life keeps going somewhere. I am in a fetal position. First it was Jake that brought me to this position. Now it's disease.

I've been named: Divorce. Dysfunction. Disease.

Jake is out of our lives more than not in these days, gone at the railroad, interrupting our new normal every eight weeks. He is adjusting to his life away from us. No pressure of family. No responsibility with kids. No taking care of the house. I've gone from the role of being a wife since sixteen to a single mother. It's a whole new landscape. One I'm trying but failing to navigate. I feel the weight of it all. I feel I don't have enough emotions, nerves, strength, time, or energy to navigate it all, to stay awake in my life. So I close my eyes to what is too big, too much.

Jake tells me I've got it easy. The kids love me and hate him. I feel guilty.

I lay on my mattress heavy with memories, tears, and silent screams. I'm locked up tight on the inside. My skin a prison.

This is now my life rhythm. I lay my head down and close my eyes and listen for Papa.

Little one, I have been on this mattress crying with you, capturing each tear, each memory. I experience all this pain with you, my love. I was with you through everything that took you under and took you down. I wrote it down and kept a record of it, even when you didn't.

My love does not manipulate you, exploiting your vulnerabilities. I do not invest my time to take, punish, or crush you. I do not pretend to love you, making demands on you to perform or else. I do not love you to control you. That is not love.

I do not keep things from you either. I do not keep you off track. I do not hold you back. I rescue. Come back to me. I'll tuck you inside my love and empower you. I give you everything you need. My love is a safe room.

My healing oil runs down into every home, every crack and crevice, every closed door. It covers floors. Doors too. It works through broken open words, glory shattering the darkness.

A new rhythm is emerging, daughter. Wait for it. Rest inside me. I have tucked you up under my wing. My love is your shade. Find rest in it. Remember the words I have said to you. Hang on to them.

forty-three

Hospital Rooms

Life is coming at me, and I can't outwork or outrun the pain anymore. Pain is winning.

I was at Office Depot when the pain rushed in, and it was more than I could handle. I doubled over, hit the floor, then realized I was out of Percocet. I called Dr. V first, and he told me to get to the emergency room at St. Joseph Medical Center. I called my mom, and she picked me up and drove straight to the hospital where I was admitted immediately.

It was as if I was in a scene in a movie. The rescue team put a tube in my chest to feed me, found a vein for the IV, and dosed me with narcotics.

It's a relief now, me laying here, left alone. There are people here if I need them, and they help me without giving me something I didn't ask for. They also don't take anything from me. They don't steal what I don't have to give. And then there are the narcotics to numb the pain of it all.

Nurses and doctors come in and out, their mouths moving, looking concerned and squeezing my hand to reassure me. I don't hear much of what they say anymore.

In the hospital, I realize I can't pray anymore, not the way I want anyway. I can only listen. I just sit on the toilet, in the bed, wherever I am, and as the pain comes in waves, all I can manage is, "God, you are more than enough." I repeat it over and over.

I have been battling this disease for five years now. I've tried everything: long-term steroids, Remicade infusions, injecting myself with Humira. All of it has made my body intolerant to the medications. Lately, even the narcotics have stopped working. I'm intolerant. Nothing kills the pain.

I'm embarrassed when Dr. V, my GI, asks me how I'm doing, if I am getting help for myself, getting safe, getting a divorce. He knows about Jake and me, knows Jake doesn't care for me in any real way. Dr. V validates my pain, my invisibleness. He has seen inside my body many times. He sees what most people do not. He knows I hide my pain—physical and emotional. He also knows I am the last in line to take care of myself. He knows my entire life is an emergency, and my sickness doesn't have my time. If I take care of myself, everyone and everything else will fall apart.

Dr. V tells me ulcers have spread up most of my colon. My body is attacking itself, and the risk of colon cancer is high. I won't make it without surgery, and he can't do anything else for me. He tells me about a brilliant GI surgeon who specializes in JPOUCH surgery, where they surgically create a J-shaped reservoir out of my small intestine as an alternate way for me to store and pass stool. They would remove my entire colon. I would wear an ostomy bag for a year and a half while I wait for my small intestine to heal, he tells me.

He thinks I am a good candidate. It's a major procedure, he says, requiring three major surgeries.

Colon cancer. Major surgery. Will I even live?

God, you're not taking away the disease or the devastation, are you? You're not fixing Jake either, are you?

Little one, I'm not fixing you either. I'm making you whole, bringing you into my family. Remember, the story is going somewhere. Your heart is set on pilgrimage. It is in all the yeses that wholeness comes.

Fifteen years, Papa. I have believed for a miracle all that time.

Last night, the night before I was admitted to the ER, before my normal would change forever, I lay looking up at the moon from the window above my bed, full and bright against the black sky. Not a star in sight. I traced it with my finger. A circle. I've run in lots of those.

I believed Jake would choose you. Choose help. I see how powerful our story could be together. If you saved a marriage like ours, you could save any marriage. But that doesn't seem to be the plan. I'm too tired to talk anymore, Papa. I want to sleep now. Before I do, though, I guess I should say my trust is all of everything I have. There isn't anywhere safe to put it anymore. I want you to have it.

In that moment, the moon melts into my hospital room, filling it with liquid warmth. It's as if I see Jesus's hand reaching through that window, into my life, all the way back through my lineage, back to the original wound. And he touches it.

I curl up in Papa's presence, loved. Safely tucked in his arms. I sleep. Safe. Papa found me. He always knows where I am.

The world is a broken system full of fallen people with heart disease. Little one, you cannot fix yourself or the people you love. You cannot fix Jake, or as painful as it is, your children.

We've got a long way to go, little one, yet we've come so far. I am in agony with you, watching you. I hurt where you hurt, ache where you ache. I stop breathing when you do. I hear your silent screams. Since the beginning, I have been watching your life unfold, cheering you on. I am here. I am waiting for you to let me help you heal. You are at the very end of yourself. Let me help you turn the corner. Let me help you make a hard right and begin to go a new way.

You are living in a fantasy world with Jake, thinking you might change him. You see what I'm showing you is true, yet you don't believe it. Hear my voice. Keep acting on it. You're not crazy, little one. You're falling over the edge, but you haven't hit the ground yet. My hands keep you suspended in midair. I wait for you to choose. And the right choice might hurt momentarily, but because of me, you will rise. I know pain, but I also know resurrection. I know healing and wholeness.

Trust me and see what miracles I can work when my children say no to many things to say yes to me.

I see your pain. I am healing you, rebuilding your house. Not only your house, my love, oh, no. My love for you knows no bounds. You can never know how deep my love is for you. Even now, I am running my finger over the circle of your life and your mother's, grandmother's, and great-grandmother's lives, reaching all back through your family lineage. I am touching the original wound, restoring it. I'm tearing down, setting you up with my gospel of put-back-togetherness. My gospel doesn't bully from the outside, beloved, it emancipates you on the inside, see?

I'm binding up broken beauty. You will no longer be broken-hearted. You will be radically resurrected at the root.

I'm binding up broken
beauty. You will no longer be
brokenhearted. You will be radically
RESURRECTED AT THE

root.

—Papa

chapter

forty-four

Tattoo

arrive at The Pearl Event dressed in a pink floral skirt and gray
T-shirt. I wear fresh ink on my forearm. I've wanted a tattoo for
years but never knew what I wanted bad enough to wear forever.
Papa gave me the word for my first tattoo—warrior.

The act of naming is significant in every God-story. Papa tells
me that when I was born my parents named me, but so did he.
He says I have always been his daughter. He named me Beloved
Warrior. I am to live from that name from now on. He has a great
adventure just for me. A mission to live out while we travel together.
He says he can use my whole life to shape me into my name.

I want to mark this moment with a tattoo, a visual reminder
that I'm not alone in writing my story anymore. That I'm no longer
an orphan who has to fend and fight for enough. That I have a Papa
who makes food, sets the table, and feeds me.

A tattoo will be a visual reminder of who I am, where I'm going,
and that I'm not alone. Because I forget. We all do.

Karen invited me to speak at The Pearl Event in Chattanooga,

Tennessee, even though I've never spoken to a group of women before.

I know it's a breadcrumb. So I take and eat. And I do what it says.

There are round tables laden with white blooms of peonies, hydrangeas, and garden roses. The tables are strewn with candles that welcome us with their flickering flames, telling us to come, rest, and warm our hearts.

I find a seat. My thoughts scurry mindlessly, like ants gathering and consuming. I make small talk with strangers at my table. I know a couple of the women through blogging, but the truth is, I don't really know them. Seeing and knowing are not the same.

Karen interrupts our talking. She tells us the day's agenda, welcomes us, and welcomes the Holy Spirit. Beckie opens our time with worship. Soon after she begins singing, something cracks my heart open. Something in the melody, the words, or maybe the air. Like a fire, a war cry rises up within me.

I'm sitting at the table between Nikki and a stranger, waiting my turn to speak. My stomach knots. I can't listen to what is being said. All I can think about is what I am going to say and how I can't talk in a straight line.

I don't know if there's a place for me with these women, but at this table, there is.

The question is asked from the worship leader: What do you want?

What do you want, little one?

I'm desperate to be known, and I don't want to settle for being seen. I want to take off my skin, my role, my social media. Is there a table where I can belong? To something other than these name tags, stereotypes, judgments, and attitudes?

I wonder if anyone else feels this way. Am I the only one? I don't want to be here, but Papa tells me he has something for me here. I'm learning it is normal to feel this way, like a misfit, when God is wanting me to eat breadcrumbs. I know if I walk through it, there is provision on the other side. Scared precedes sacred. Deep down, I want to save myself. It feels uncomfortable, selfish, prideful. I know I can't save myself anymore, and somehow, when I take and eat his words, I trust Papa is helping me.

When I'm not under pressure, I know these women, too, are anxious. They feel their story isn't as good as others', isn't perfect, even if their social media makes it appear that way. More than likely, they feel very much like me. They feel like they don't have it all together either.

Maybe they want permission to put all of their heart on the table. Just like me. Isn't that what tables are for? A table is a place where we don't let vulnerability keep us armored up, living life like there isn't enough for each of us.

What if I could give permission to us all and go straight to the heart?

A voice interrupts my contemplation.

I watch each woman take her turn speaking. I wait my turn. Karen invites me up, pulls me in for a hug, and champions me with her words. I try and believe those words as I walk up the three steps, microphone in one hand, journal in the other.

Unable to comprehend my notes, I open my mouth, but my words are jumbled. I can't find the story line in my notes. I silently beg the audience—anyone—to help me as I stand here losing my place, maybe losing face too. The abuse from Jake has left my heart and mind with a limp. My mind doesn't work like it used to.

I can't say the word *abuse* yet. I haven't freed myself from the lie that abuse is defined only as physical abuse. I haven't been hit, shoved, or slapped. But what about emotional, sexual, spiritual abuse? This has been my experience, but I have not named it yet.

My story is a web of deception so deep that I will never find my way out. Ever! I think they believe I am something I'm not. They see my Instagram and know I'm the House of Belonging founder, but I feel like an imposter. Wait until they find out I couldn't care for my children . . .

All of a sudden, I don't want to be here. I don't want to be judged. I don't want to feel like a project to be fixed. I feel shame pinning my arms against the wall, putting a hand over my mouth. Putting me in my place.

I watch Papa, though, working the room. I sense his love. He is my rescue. I'll trust him. I may not be a good speaker, but I am a truth-teller. Truth is telling me to stay standing, laying all of my heart on the table. Maybe it will give everyone else permission to do the same.

So I push my way through the talk, pouring out my story in a room full of strangers, leaning my full weight on God. As I pour out the pain of some of the things that have taken me under, run me over, run me down, and run me through, the women listen.

There's not enough time to tell the whole story, not all of it. And shame keeps me from sharing about leaving my children. Today, it feels just like yesterday. For twenty-five years the words "What kind of mother does that?" have been buried alive.

Six words that have been my name.

But what kind of mother goes back? This is how Papa answers me at The Pearl Event. *The kind of mother who goes back says, "Restore me." The kind of mother who does the hard and holy work of letting me restore her heart, her life. She lets me give her health back, then lets me teach her how to steward her wholeness. I am making you well. Are you ready? You will no longer be able to use shame as your name anymore. How? By taking me at my word because you have no other option.*

When the day is over, Rebekah Lyons comes to me, says she has watched me living my life through my Instagram posts. She was an outsider reading my Instagram like a book. She saw me barely getting above the pain, then going back under. This is how Rebekah read my story.

I ask Rebekah if she will pray with me. She has me gather a few women I want around me, and we go into a room. I see other women coming in, one by one, as they circle me like a pack of warrior women. They stand on the front line for me, carrying me.

This feels something like family. Hearts knotted together in our messes. Holding hands. Crying out to God together. Face to face. Side by side. For each other. With each other.

The sound of our prayers, the laying of hands on each other, it makes a way for us all, lifting and turning our hearts to him. This prayer is sweet water, and it quenches our thirst.

I am giving you the words to your story, making the invisible visible. In all circumstances I am giving you what's missing, giving back what shame robbed. I am pushing you into a new place, not returning you to something. I continue to use words to push you out of the miry clay of your past, into a brand-new woman you've never before seen.

Little one, I don't repair and reinstate. I don't fix what isn't broken in you. I restore. I'm creating an opening for you to welcome the discomfort of another way. Will you say yes? Restoration, my love, is not returning to what was. Restoration is me creating something new. I can restore anyone if they will say yes to a new and often raw and uncomfortable pathway.

You are a warrior who is learning she is on pilgrimage in a story that is bigger than hers. You are a generational wrecking ball, a forerunner who dares to break out of family chaos for her children and children's children until Jesus comes. You are a woman who is learning that belonging means following Jesus. You can hang everything on Jesus because he hung his everything for you on the cross.

Keep trusting me to prove myself faithful. Keep focused on the interior, the place I live and speak with you. I am giving you a new language, new thoughts, new ways. Keep looking up. My gaze is always locked on you.

*You are
a warrior*

who is learning she is on pilgrimage in

a story that is bigger than hers. You are

a generational wrecking ball, a forerunner

who dares to break out of family chaos

for her children and children's

children until Jesus comes.

–Papa

forty-five

Stone Cottage

know I'm supposed to be here in Franklin, Tennessee, but I can't explain why I'm here. It feels like a mystery to solve. One of picking up and eating breadcrumbs. God made a way and said run, and that's what I did.

My friend Karen and I leave the downtown Franklin Starbucks where we meet for coffee before I drive back home to Missouri in a few days. We must be crazy walking outside in the Tennessee heat that will melt skin from bones. But we do. We want to chat more, but James, Karen's one-year-old, is fussy.

We walk past Frothy Monkey. Karen spots a for rent sign on a house up ahead. Now I'm standing on the step of a front door. I knock on the door, but no one answers.

"It's unlocked," I tell Karen.

Karen cheers me to "Open it, girl! Go in!"

I step into a quaint stone cottage in the heart of downtown Franklin, Tennessee. Karen and I walk in and split in different directions, exploring, calling out what we see. "The kitchen's been redone," I say.

It's a two-bedroom with a staircase to a loft with a small living area and a third bedroom alcove. That bedroom is perfect for Grace.

Nikki and I could have the two bedrooms downstairs. My heart wants to believe this is where I could be, but fear tells me my credit is ruined, reminds me I've been told no before. This will be a no too.

Karen's voice interrupts my internal dialogue.

"This is in Williamson County School District, a good school for Grace. This is perfect for you. You can walk to shops and restaurants," Karen says.

Yes, but I'm listening to the sound of the house, listening for the sound of Papa's voice, I think, smiling.

I leave her praying over my would-be bedroom, walk into the kitchen, and I peer at the back door, captivated by the dreamy yard. It's fenced and cozy with a small covered porch perfect for a fire, lights, and God-stories.

I walk back into the kitchen feeling like I broke in (which we did), and I see a business card on the counter. I pick it up, and Karen tells me to call the number. "Really? Do you want me to call it?" I have a habit of fumbling words when I talk.

I call, afraid, and a man picks up. "Go in, the door is open," he says. I confess, with relief, that we already did. He says his email is on the card and to shoot him a quick email, and he will send me the application. My heart bends into a sigh. This is too good to be true.

I hang up the phone and tell Karen that God seems to be dropping more breadcrumbs. Sometimes I choose to eat them; sometimes I don't. Today I do. My blood, thick with doubt, begins to move hot as I toy with the thought. Could I really move here?

When I get in the car, I call Nikki and Grace, telling them about the house Papa found for us. I fill out the online app and wait, hearing nothing for two days. I argue with myself about whether it would be trusting God to email and check in. I finally cave and email the landlord. I tell him I am more than a credit score and its history. Please meet me first before you tell me no. He calls me, asking if I can meet him tomorrow at 1:00 p.m.

I pull into the drive; a group of people welcomes me. His mom, Carol, who is a realtor, and also his wife and two children. I tell them a piece of my story the best I can.

They agree to let me have the house, but say I need to give a double deposit. I write a check, and it is like pushing all my chips into the middle of the table. I have no credit to get a loan to get us by if this goes south.

Two days later, Grace, Nikki, my mom, who had spent the last two weeks with us, and I drive back to Missouri with a secret. I stop in Frothy Monkey on the way out to grab a latte and a snicker-doodle, then I hit I-65. As I drive I say a silly goodbye out loud to downtown Franklin, saying, "I'll see you soon," my heart spilling over in excitement until I'm snapped back to reality. I have to tell the kids I'm moving to Tennessee. Tell them I won't be working at the shop anymore.

I talk to myself all the way back to Missouri. I'm looking for breadcrumbs like road signs.

Chelsee, Phillip, and my five grandbabies recently moved back from Florida after two and a half years. Reece moved into our shop around the same time. He hasn't been a part of the family since he was a teenager. I thought Papa's promise to me in Isaiah that all my children would come back was coming true. For the first time, all five of my kids live by me. We are together.

Just when I thought things were coming together, Tennessee disrupted.

I know I can say no. That would make the kids feel okay. I wouldn't have to feel their afraids. But I know *I* won't be okay. I know how this goes. I've been doing it for forty-seven years. I choose me. Not in the way I chose me when I gave my children to Ronnie. This is different. My kids are grown adults now. Except Grace; she is fifteen. I want to keep eating breadcrumbs. I want to follow the trail. I want Grace to experience Papa like I do. I want her to see for herself. I want all my kids to see for themselves.

I don't want to numb myself. But I can hardly feel their emotions. I feel extremely exposed and fragile.

Things have gotten better at home except for Jake and me. We just hang in midair, years of loose ends unresolved. I fear losing my dream of God restoring us. Our kids. And I fear losing our insurance. Am I making the biggest mistake of my life? What am I doing? Do I dare to risk everything? I want the kids to be okay. I want to be okay. Is the pull to go of my own imagination?

Indecision swings me left, then right. This is a big move.

Look what God is doing! I can hardly contain the hope that I carry, but in order to take him at his word, I have to act on it, scared. I have no other choice, really. I can stay where I'm at and live in the what if for the rest of my life. Or I can take God at his word, and if I fail according to human standards, then I fail. At the very least, if I fail, I will have no regret.

231

I am uncovering it all, my love. I have gone ahead. Always been ahead. I have stood here in this house, have seen you walking through.

My love, I am leading you to a table. A table of words. Words that make meals prepared by my hands. My words are always working. I use my words in the best possible way. I love preparing the best meals you've ever had. I love inviting you into this ancient table fellowship. As intimate as a table for two—for you and me. But soon, my love, I'll ask you to come with me, partner with me to set tables long and wide. Feed others my words. Tell God-stories. Remember me around tables. Remember my faithfulness. It is remembering that moves you forward. This is your something-more, little one. This is where you eat from at every point in our journey home.

The story we are writing, little one, is one of restoration of family and home, and it is happening around my table. I am leading you out of an old way into a new way. Follow me, little one. I know the way. I am the way. My way is easy and light. We travel light, little one, not loaded down with stuff. We are going places.

I made you a warrior to stand against pressure, the pressure of returning to the old and familiar ways of destruction. To stand and push back against the enemy. To stand up and fight for your family, your home, your community. I am making a new space for you and your family. Together we are breaking down generational patterns that have broken down your family lineage.

Someday your children, grandchildren, and great-grandchildren will say, "I want to be just like her." Look back in my words and read how I never failed my children.

I don't take people apart and put them back together only to take them all apart again. I make it whole at the center of your interior. My breadcrumbs, a home, a table—these are all my gifts for you.

Together we are breaking down generational patterns that have (broken) down your family lineage.

—Papa

forty-six

Leaving

L eaving the kids after we are all living in the same town again feels like abandoning them all over again. I'm leaving the only place I had a shape in. I am risking everything that feels comfortable, but Papa is telling me I must go.

Grace and I pack all our belongings in one moving cube. I leave the rest of our things for Chelsee, Phillip, and the grandbabies. They are taking over my lease.

Grace and I pull out of the driveway. The day is all sun. I am all sad. Chelsee stays downstairs, not able to say goodbye. Nikki walks out with us. She's coming down to live with us in a couple months. We wave until we can't see each other anymore. Sobs try climbing up and out of my heart, but I tell them no. Not today. This is a God thing. I hold my hand up to those thoughts, telling them to stop.

Then I open my heart to Papa's voice, saying yes to his words.

Grace and I drive across an invisible state line, into light and unknown territory between my home in Missouri and this new one in Tennessee. In the rearview mirror is my old life. As I watch it fade, I see pain like years, being pushed back into history. I hear Papa say, *Only remember to live forward.*

I did it! I actually did it. I am moving to a new state. A new life. Starting from scratch, aren't I? I smile, understanding the vision more clearly now. I used to run five miles a day on the treadmill. I saw myself as the superhero, the kids on my cape. I would carry them on my back as I flew.

Now I'm seeing that I am not a superhero. The weight of them on my back caused it to break. I'm not made to carry my children, or anyone.

I feel Papa put his arm around me. *My love, saying yes to this is how you are making a way for your children. By saying yes to me and yourself. Letting me rescue you. Letting me write your story. Together. You and I are turning the table on the enemy.*

I smile at Papa. *I can almost hear the dinner bell, Papa. I smell home.*

I don't know how it feels or looks to not walk bent over broken. I knew my shape when I was in Missouri. I don't know much of how anything will be in Tennessee. I do know that I will keep my heart open. I will eat Papa's breadcrumbs wherever they may fall. *I don't know where I'm going, Papa. I'm taking you at your word.*

I've cut the last string that ties Jake and me together: provision. I've told him I'm not taking any more of his money. I've told him I am moving to Tennessee. He asks if I'm leaving him. I say yes. It feels like I'm fighting Satan himself to pack my life inside a moving cube. I used to dream God could put us back together, put our family back together. Now I'm like a wild horse running on hallowed ground, running toward a finish line I can't see.

Papa asks me to trust him. He tells me I'm running toward

something bigger. I know God is a big God. This is good, because I'm in a big mess. So I roll the car windows down and throw my will out the window. *Your will, not mine.* I take faith with both hands and decide to believe God is present in this mess with me.

Grace and I look at each other, read each other's minds, and smile. What are we doing? We are really doing this! She puts headphones on and goes to sleep.

I settle in for the ten-hour drive.

I am so proud of you.

I have plans for you. I always have. You have opened the book of your heart to my gaze. I am rewriting your story. My living words found you; here they are between the pages of my story. You've followed the maps, the ways of escape, and most importantly the medicine. My gospel of put-back-togetherness.

You hear the sound and feel the rhythm of the swing of liberty, little one. You've always heard. There is an appointed time for everything under the sun. I am behind the scenes working, making ways. You listen with more than your ears. You hear with your heart, feel rhythms with your heart.

Trust me, little one. You hear my voice. Trust it and run.

I always go before you, and I know it will not unpack like you think it might. That's okay. Still search. Don't stop searching my heart, for my heartland is yours. I have already given it to you. Keep digging; in your pain you will find treasures of pleasure instead of the pain.

Let me be your faithful partner, providing with no strings. I am free—call me and see. Call me once and over and over.

forty-seven

Safe Bed

It's late and I can barely keep my eyes open. I push my notebooks and Bible to the other side of the bed where Jake used to sleep. I go into the bathroom to wash off my makeup. I stare at the woman in the mirror. I see the years in the lines around her eyes. It's been 348 days since I moved from my house in Missouri, since I escaped my life and left behind the pain of that place.

I slide between the sheets, pull the covers up, and turn off the lamp. The only light is from the moon. Its fullness falls through my window. I am alone in my own bedroom in my own bed. I am alone in the dark with Papa.

The memory bursts in unannounced: Jake saying to me our bodies fit together perfectly, and he was right. When he hugged me, our bodies fit at all the right spots. The top of my head rested just at his heart. I could hear his heartbeat when we hugged. It wasn't all bad, was it?

Now that the door is open, I can't seem to shut it. More memories are not far behind. Like the time Jake drove twelve hours from

Minnesota so he could be with me while I was in withdrawal from narcotics. I needed his arms. Something warm that could hold me. Something to keep me from falling over the edge of life.

I miss his arms that held me. I miss having someone to lie with me. I need someone to tell me I'm okay, to tell me I'm going to make it through this. Someone to tell me it's not too late, that I'm not too old. It feels like I'm not going to make it in this new land. Tonight, I feel like a ghost in Tennessee.

I roll over, pulling the covers over my head, and cry into my pillow.

I wonder whether he is with someone else. Does he think of me anymore? Surely he couldn't forget me after twenty-three years of life together. If I call him, he will come. He always comes when I'm needy. We'll pick up for another quarter of a century. I'm too old to find love anyway. There isn't much time left.

I hear some ghost under my bed whisper, "Call him." I want to feel something, anything but emptiness. I remember the feeling of Jake's arms pulling me into his shape where I fit perfectly. I question how a love that feels so good can sometimes play out so bad. I know it'd only take a phone call, but I also know it would kill me on the inside. There isn't a peace yet. I don't sense I've put my finger on my something-more just yet. I'm supposed to keep going.

The drive to be in any shape other than the one you have for me, Papa, is disappearing.

I think of how sick I was. How my mind selects only the highlights. I have selective amnesia.

Papa, you're here and you are too real, and I know what you've told me to do. I know that you've told me to get away from him, haven't you?

I sense I'm in a battle. I roll over and push play on my phone, lyrics from "Good Good Father" turning me around, keeping me from following my thoughts down a rabbit hole.

You're not going back. I'm restoring you. Wait and see. Stay with me, little one. I'm here. Follow me. Watch and see. I'm working.

I am wide-awake, Papa. I feel you, your words inside me. I find them, touch them. I hang on to them.

I sing into the night, "You're a good, good father, and I'm loved by you." The weight of memories lifts. The weight of Papa's glory is heavier in my room tonight.

The moon isn't bright enough tonight to chase the lies away, but Papa's tender whisper of love in the dead of night is. I shape my pile of pillows into a person by tucking them behind me, turning on my side, and snuggling into them. I imagine these pillows are his words. Papa's words spoon me. I pull him in and around me tonight. I let his words hold me.

I sense Papa's presence beside me. I pull out my heart and hand it to him to take care of it while I sleep. My thoughts are too much for me but not for him.

"Look how far we've come, Papa," I whisper. I think about my journey. Remembering turns into rejoicing, and tears fall as I remember how I am learning to live loved. It isn't all about me; it's about Papa. Even though I am now in a new place, my heart carries all of me in it. I still carry Missouri inside me. I miss my kids. And my grandkids. I wonder if I will ever get to be a hands-on grandma. I'm like a tree pulled from the ground, hanging in midair, roots untethered from earth. The adrenaline of leaving is wearing off. My life and business are changing fast. I don't have time to be still.

Little one, you're okay. Now I have space to begin.

I feel him smile.

As clear as day, I hear him say, *Talk to me about your day, your fears, and the new ideas you have. Talk to me about the kids, the grandbabies, and your aches and pains. Dream with me. Make lists with me. I want to hear everything. Hold nothing back.*

As sleep finds me, new skin grows over a wound.

I ask nothing of you, little one. Nothing but that you listen to me and rest in me. You have everything you need to be strong. I am using all things to make you strong, like steel. Soon you will be able to stand on your own two feet. You don't know how powerful you are, my love. I am bringing you healing. It is harder to stay free than it is to get free, but together we are doing it. We are recovering all your pieces, the pieces you thought you lost. I am so proud of you, little one. I'm telling all of heaven, "Look at my girl! Look at her. She keeps getting up, keeps fighting the good fight. She's doing hard and holy work!"

I am creating a *new place* of safety. You are not returning to what was lost. I am not taking you back to a sentimental place as you dream it to be. I am pushing you into a new safe place. A land that lives within you, a place you feel very uncomfortable in because it doesn't seem like return. Because it isn't. Trying to understand, trying to look at it from your limited understanding, you think it should be. But my restoration can never be return because the wounds of past identity are inconsolable. I am allowing life to push you into a new land, a land that lives within you. Over time you will see it isn't about you, your circumstances, or a place. It is about me and my people. It isn't about arriving. My restoration happens inside you. My words are finding *you*.

Take and eat.

I am so proud of you, little one. I'm telling all of

heaven,

"Look at my girl! Look at her. She keeps getting up, keeps fighting the good fight."

—Papa

forty-eight

Like a Sonic Boom

The phone rings at 4:00 a.m. It's Chelsee. She's crying and I already know this is a call I will never forget. Ronnie is dead, she says. Just like that, he is gone. Fifty years old. Sudden heart attack.

Shock slams my emotions through ice.

"What?" I say. My voice doesn't sound like me.

My only thoughts are for my kids, who are in Missouri while I'm here in Tennessee. It doesn't dawn on me that my first love, the man I don't have closure with, the man I never apologized to, is gone. On the plane to Missouri, the lack of closure breaks over me. I weep through it all.

The day of the funeral arrives, and we drive to the gravesite. The black cars wind through the hills of Boone County like a kingsnake headed to his home.

I can't stop thinking of his last thoughts when he was dying.

It haunts me. It isn't fair. My kids' dad died without them having closure with him either. He took that hurt with him too.

There is a welcome mat here for me today: his brothers, their wives, even his mom. But during the service I stand back. I don't go up and see him. I sit in the back with the grandkids and let the kids grieve. If we were still married today, I would have been a widow!

I know he loved me. He never remarried until three years ago.

What do we know this side of heaven? How will this play out? How will you ever be able to restore any of this, God? The yes I said when I left everything here to follow you isn't looking like I thought it might.

Everything hurts. Everything burns.

The world doesn't care that someone died from this life; it just keeps spinning. Questions break speed barriers like a sonic boom. Can all of the world stop for a moment of silence, of respect? Please, please stop.

I stop. I stay. I'm breathing for you in the moments you can't find your breath, little one. I'm giving your family word-to-word resuscitation. My army angels, like giant sequoias, are lined up along the street, standing at attention as you and the kids wind your way through Boone County. Do you see them? Feel them? I am making the enemy pay for everything he has stolen, killed, and destroyed from you, your children, and your family. I give you my word.

You are held.

forty-nine

Wrestling

After the funeral I go back to Tennessee.

The business is doing well, but pressure is mounting. When I first came to Tennessee, I didn't see signs like ours anywhere in downtown. Now folks are copying the signs and the storefront I opened is proving harder than I thought. I back out of the Franklin, Tennessee, storefront when I sense Papa tapping me on the shoulder, saying not now. In a knee-jerk decision, Nikki opens a storefront in Missouri only to find out it has an undisclosed sewer gas leak. The House of Belonging was built on cash, not credit. I don't have credit to get a loan. Money once sitting in our account is now leaking out, and I can't plug the holes. I sense something unknown, something big coming. I don't know what it is, not yet. It is like ominous clouds, clouds like fists squeezing the life out of me and the kids. Out of the business even. To try and stop what I've known in my heart for twenty years. God's promises. Promises to me. To my kids. To my family. Restoration.

During all of this, Nikki had said yes to adopting from China, and the House of Belonging is helping to fund that adoption. What if the business folds? Will we be able to bring little Etta home to our table? To Papa's table?

I have so much to process. I take the weekend to write with Papa. To listen for what he is saying and to wait for him to feed me. I spend the weekend looking up. I ask him if I made a mistake in coming to Tennessee. Maybe I'm supposed to go back home? I let it all out. The disappointment, questions, and the what ifs.

I still wrestle with the orphan in me. But I know God won't let it all fall apart. My head knows I am his daughter; my heart just needs to catch up sometimes. I am learning to lean on Papa's arm, letting him walk me down the grand ballroom steps of life and lead me in the dance of life.

It feels as if he is gently divorcing me from the world. *Is that what this is, Papa? Am I on this journey so I can learn beyond a shadow of a doubt whom I belong to?* I feel his assurance that there will be no more vacillating when we are done. *My heart is okay as long as I keep looking at you, right, Papa?* Circumstances are producing a vacuum effect—sucking resources like a tidal wave, exposing my heart like the bottom of a seafloor. *All I know to do is keep eating your words, Papa.* I need to keep trusting, following the breadcrumbs as an act of worship.

I can't sing to save my life. Never carried a tune. But I'm learning that there is a singing a heart does that moves God's heart. I don't think worship is only singing out loud in a group of people at church. To me, worship is a language. A heart-language. Worship is my language now.

I worship my way through days. It is the sound of my ram's horn.

My battle cry becomes all the promises you've given me. Instead of letting circumstances bully me, I dig deeper into your words. I sound with my mouth who you say I am. I say it over and over until it becomes stone-cold reality. There is power in my mouth and my heart when they both say yes.

Little one, look with me. I am making you ready.

When you eat my words, it creates something within. These are living letters. Clauses. Sentences. Pages and chapters. These are living letters, leading you into *shalom*. Let them lead you into deep peace. Into intimacy with me where your heart can live naked and unashamed.

I am rebuilding your life from the rubble. I am using it all to restore you, to make you whole. I am giving you full life. Even in all the empty places. I give you the kind of fullness you can have anytime you want it. It's free, stringless. It isn't dependent on you, on others, your circumstances, your mess. Just pull up a chair, little one. Just let me love you.

And you don't need to worry about all these hard parts of the journey. I am going to give you everything you lost, in a piece-by-piece healing. Pull up a chair and see what I will do.

fifty

Ancient Longings

O ver scrambled eggs and coffee, Rebekah tells me about a study she's doing. She says the teacher is so good. I would love her. The recent lesson reminded her of me. It was the woman with the alabaster jar, the one who washed Jesus's feet with her tears and anointed them with perfume. She asks if I want to come with her.

I can't, I tell her. I'm heading back to Missouri for a couple of weeks. We continue on with our conversation, and I don't give a second thought to the Bible study.

Weeks later, for no reason, I remember Rebekah's invitation. I text her, asking her if there is another class. She says there is. In fact, it is tonight, and she asks whether I want her to come with me. Of course! My insides shake with anxious hope. It's a bread-crumb! I'm learning that even though the landscape has changed, Papa is still leading me with these breadcrumbs. The land is new; the promise is not.

I pull into the parking lot of Church of the City. I'm hungry for a go or a stay. Am I to go back to Missouri? Or stay here in Tennessee?

It has been a year of watching House of Belonging change, something dying and something else being born. I have been going back and forth for almost two years now. Every six weeks. Staying for one to three weeks. I'm not here, not there. I'm suspended in a plot twist.

I need a home base—not necessarily a house, but a people. Not flatterers and dissemblers, rather people who know God's story is going somewhere and that those who follow Jesus are going there too. People who don't avert their eyes from pain and suffering. People who have been through hell and made it out the other side but don't forget the ones coming behind them. People who stay in the trenches of life not because they don't know how to get out but to feed people and help pull them out. People who don't use others as steps up their own ladder but help by doing life side by side. Face to face. So they know they aren't doing life alone.

In expectation, I arrive early and find a shady parking spot. I turn the car off, pull down the visor mirror, rummage through my purse, and find my lipstick. I look in the mirror, and I know I'm lacking. Why does being in this town with its churches and pretty people some days leave me feeling like I'm in junior high gym class?

I finish putting on my lipstick and tell the girl in the mirror she is okay. Stay open, real, and don't try and get yourself together. Just get inside and find out what God has for you.

From the car I watch women begin to arrive and walk in.

I recall what brought me here, to this parking lot. My heart growls like a hungry stomach, somehow knowing what's being served. Papa nudges me to open the car door and get going.

I've got another breadcrumb waiting, little one.

I walk into the church unrehearsed. Another room full of women and tables.

There are twelve round tables and the low hum of women's voices sharing, laughing, and loving. There is a sense of safe in this space. Some lean into deep conversations. Others stand in groups of three or four, laughing. A few sit alone looking at their phones. I look for Rebekah. She isn't here yet. I practice not overthinking and just pick a seat and sit somewhere. There's a woman already at the table, and we each say polite hellos.

Rebekah texts, says she's running late, and my nerves jump. Sometimes I feel unprotected, like walking in here alone. It is still painfully raw to not have a person to hide behind, like a husband or a mom. People seeing me hurts my nerves, my emotions. It seems like a weakness, a disorder, something to be fixed. But I don't think it is.

I hear Papa's reassurance. *You're okay, little one.*

Kristi, the teacher, spots me, makes a beeline my way, and hugs me like I have never been hugged. Not even by my mother or father. Her hug startles something deep in me.

"Welcome, welcome everyone," she begins. "Thank you all for coming. For saying no to other things so you can say yes to God tonight. How many of you would rather hear from God than me tonight? Raise your hands!"

I raise mine.

The classroom becomes a sanctuary. Kristi explains the class, and as she does, I realize this is unlike any study I've been to. Kristi says it is a twelve-week biblical feast, a meal we don't have to prepare ourselves. God has already prepared the best meal we will ever have. This is the next new thing. I posture myself to take and eat.

Kristi begins teaching, and I can't stop crying as she teaches about the woman at the well. She teaches the stories in a way I've never heard. She teaches through the lens of the culture of the Middle East, where the Bible was written and lived out. Suddenly, the Bible goes from black and white to living color.

This is the God I've come to know through following, eating—and then doing—breadcrumbs. God intervened when nobody else would or could.

All I see are faces, luminous and lit with hunger. And they're not hungry for Kristi's personality but for what Jesus is serving at the table, stories of women and Jesus. Papa's breath blows his words tonight, and they become living bread, the Bread that walked among us, breaking off pieces of himself. Feeding us. Feeding me. Meeting each of us where we are, wherever that is.

The table is his Word. He is at the head, with us, and he tells me I belong at his table. Yes, I am a misfit. This world is not supposed to feel like home. I am not to belong to it. I am to belong to him.

He tells me he can give me living water and bread that will heal me. He can take my pain, shame, and all the things I'm still carrying.

It feels like I've fought against the call on my life. Maybe my purpose too. There are so many names for it. But it feels like a hard life, an abusive relationship, and my own sick heart have taken my something-more from me. But I sense I'm as close as I've ever been before. Like I'm getting to the end of a great story, devouring page after page to read the last chapter. But I know if I hurry or read the last page first, I'll miss everything in between. I keep eating breadcrumbs, knowing they are leading me but feeling lost in a lifetime of waiting. I thought I didn't belong anywhere, that I was crazy, fatally flawed, and that I should keep my mouth shut. That I was embarrassing everyone. That I make people uncomfortable with the way God made me. But if I can grab my something-more with both hands, I will finally fit in, even if that isn't how I expected it to look.

You don't embarrass me, Papa tells me. *And though you've kept that thought inside you for forty-eight years, it's time to let me hold that hurt. Can you hear me? I am a table, a feast for you. And I'm going to lead you somewhere new, to a new table. You don't have a map to that table. Follow me. I'll be the map. My words are signs.*

I don't know what this means, but somehow, I know where the new land is. *I am going to go to Israel, aren't I, Papa?* I hadn't even looked at the cards on the table, but I do now. I pick one up. It's an invitation to Israel.

My story is going somewhere, little one. We are on pilgrimage. Say yes?

I nearly run to my car holding the yes in my heart until I can unpack what has just happened. God has given me direction. He wants me to travel, to find him at a new table. This is what I was born for! *Where did that come from?* I ask myself.

Travel—why does travel cause my heart to pay attention?

You're made for this.

For what, Papa?

You belong to me. Together we will excavate you, a lifelong adventure of peeling away layers! Unforced rhythms of peeling away layers and transforming you from one image to another—to mine.

The deepest part of my core erupts; this is what I was born for!

I am dizzy with that discovery. Even though I don't know what *that* is yet. I know to take, eat, and do. He will show me the way.

I want to spend every day taking God at his words, doing them with courage, grace, and grit. I want to become the story my children, grandchildren, and great-grandchildren read. And after reading the end, I want them to say, "I want to be just like Grandma. I want to take God at his word, just like my mom, just like Grandma." I want to flip the script in my family story.

I know I'll need new luggage. Then Papa speaks to me about my old emotional baggage. It's been so heavy all these years. But I didn't have a safe place to unpack it, so I carried it. Now I've found a place to unpack the boxes. I am finding women who will help. I've found a place where Papa meets me. I can unpack all my hurt here, and maybe I can start healing too.

There is something dying—the old you. The new you is being born. Something new is coming. Let me be your guide. I am putting my house of belonging inside you. I am bringing order to your chaos, little one. Your life is built on belonging to me, but not by the world's definition of belonging.

I am not going to give you just a couple of people to travel with. You think that would be good enough. I'm giving you a new family to caravan with, to help write into your story, and you will write into theirs. You will learn what it looks like to create your life inside my home. I will teach you how to be a keeper and helper of people, like I've been keeping and helping you. I'll teach you how to set a table for them.

And while we're at this table, look back at your life. It's about the journey, my love, not so much the rights and wrongs, the passes or fails. It's what you are learning about me, about home, family, this table, and the gospel of put-back-togetherness.

Let me help you go deeper into our home. Use this place, Tennessee, to learn what home looks like.

And, little one, know this: I am deconstructing your kingdom for mine. The one inside you. The old has passed away, the new has come.

We are setting a table in my house of belonging. My table, in our house. And you belong here. It's that simple, really. *You belong.*

I am reordering your life. Come with me, escape from oppression, and enter into a sacred adventure where life is lived in true belonging.

My words are actual, visceral, and right now! I am not up there, out there somewhere. I am imminent and near. Right here in your now. Looking at you eye to eye and face to face. Do you hear me? You belong. Let no one say otherwise.

And little one,
know this: I am
deconstructing your
kingdom for mine.
The one inside you.
The old has passed
away, the new has come.
—Papa

fifty-one

Misfit Table

I left Kristi's class with ancient longings beating loudly in my heart. I can't shake the feeling that this is what I was born for. *Where did that come from, Papa?*

It is morning. I'm sitting outside watching the sun stream into the day. I don't know where to start, so I open my Bible to Luke 14 and ask God to help me.

God, clear the deck for me right now. Take all my cares, everything pressing on me, vexing me, weighing me down. Whatever is crooked, whatever needs to be straightened, whatever is up, down, and all around, I am laying them all out on the table. Open me. Posture me to receive. God, I am not an orphan, fatherless, needing to open the Bible to dig something out to feed myself. I have a high and holy Father who is ready, willing, and able to feed me the Holy Writ in the very way I need it right now. I'm pulling up a chair right now to the table of your words. Words that are visceral. Words that are right now. You know me by my name, Papa. Will you meet me here?

The story opens with the imagery of breakfast on a seashore,

Jesus cooking breakfast on the morning he restores Peter. This breakfast comes after Peter's three denials of Christ, after Christ's resurrection. God is resetting the deck.

Maybe this is my restoration breakfast too? As I read, twenty years of my life begin to make some sense. Years of what I thought were circles of insanity were perhaps circle patterns led by the Shepherd.

I see the word *misfit* in Luke 14 of the Message version. This chapter is titled "Invite the Misfits." In it Jesus says, "The next time you put on a dinner, don't just invite your friends and family and rich neighbors, the kind of people who will return the favor. Invite some people who never get invited out, the misfits from the wrong side of the tracks. You'll be—and experience—a blessing. They won't be able to return the favor, but the favor will be returned—oh, how it will be returned!—at the resurrection of God's people" (Luke 14:12–14 MSG).

The word *misfit* usually carries a negative connotation, but today God opens my eyes to its real meaning. A true disciple is one who leaves everything and follows Jesus, who eats his words and does what they say. Someone like that will never fit in with the world. Maybe being a misfit is just about being a pilgrim, someone who is following God in a world that does not understand.

I notice how Jesus wants to invite the common people, not the rich or religious. Not the celebrities of the day. He wants the poor, the sinners. Isn't that whom Jesus came for? Those who know their need? I know mine.

Maybe misfits are people like me who have been pushed against the wall of life by hard and hurtful things, who feel pushed out by a world that tells them they don't belong. And maybe misfits are exactly whom Jesus has saved a seat for.

After reading Luke, about Jesus breaking religion's rules, setting tables, restoration breakfasts, and misfit dinner parties, gospel-fire spreads through my veins. *What is this, Papa? What are you doing? What if I set a table, Papa, like the one in Luke 14? What if I invited the misfits like me? And asked Kristi to teach us about ancient tables, about the gospel from a Middle Eastern lens?*

I can't make sense of this, but I will ask. I text Kristi: Would you come and teach the Bible at a table? We will serve a meal around a fire. I briefly tell her about my morning with Papa.

She said this sounds like gospel. Yes! She hears it too, sees it too.

My heart bursts into flames as Papa brings full circle what I could never do on my own. He is lifting and turning my heart in a new direction.

Remember when you raised your hands of faith and said yes to me when I asked in Isaiah 6, who will go for me?

Tears stream down my face as something inside me begins to burn. *Has it been twenty years since that moment, Papa?*

I hear the question again. *Who will go for me?* This time I have twenty years of ground and a map. I think back over it all before being so quick to answer.

Are you willing to take up your cross daily? Are you willing to let everything burn to follow me?

This exchange is taking place on my deck in the early morning while cars wake up slowly, taking people to jobs, the sun slowly rising above the Tennessee hills to my left. My heart is laid naked at the table God has set for me this morning. I let him look at my motives, my whys.

Here I am, Papa. Send me.

Go, little one. Show and tell. Make it plain. I will make the way bigger and bigger as you go. We will go together. I will teach you what to say. I will put my words in your mouth. Everywhere you go, I go. In every circumstance that finds you and pushes you down, I'm already there. You are never in it alone.

I don't know how long I stay on the deck this morning. I want to keep following Papa's breadcrumbs. It has been a long time since I've eaten breadcrumbs like these.

From a Sabbath meal with religious leaders to a dinner party for misfits, Jesus broke down social barriers. He came for the misfit in us all, and he came for the Pharisee too. The Pharisee in me.

I love your Word, Papa. I love how holistic it is. How generous you are. I love that your love is bottomless. That you search us out.

The last twenty years have been a wilderness, a testing, and a sacred adventure, a story of restoration to bring me face to face with my something-more. I'm learning what my name is and what I'm made for. Sacred adventure is finding me again.

At the breakfast on the beach, Jesus was watching the fire, the fish, and his disciples. And I know he watches me the same way. Like he watched Peter at breakfast on the seashore, on the other side of his betrayal. Jesus still offers him a meal, still offers him a fresh invitation, like always. Today I'm having breakfast with Jesus. I need to be more than forgiven; I need to be restored to wholeness.

God, remove my shame, pull it up by the root, wash my heart with your words. Scrub it. Replace it with your righteousness and my rightful name, the name I'm known by. The name you called me when you swaddled me with your words when you caught me the day I entered this world.

Every day is new. Every day I get to wake up into Papa's finding-love. I get to allow him to find me. To come get me. I get to show my life as a story of who God is and what he is like. Our God-stories are like fingerprints—one of a kind. Now I get to write the greatest love story ever written. Mine.

I know the heaviness will come again, but now I know to cry out, come get me, Papa! And he will come running, lift me up, lay me across his shoulders, and carry me. I will let him. I am forever found.

When I was born, I was hurled out into a world unfamiliar to me. It was not mine. I instinctively knew it. My mom pushed me out, and I have fought to find my way home ever since—not back inside her womb but into my heavenly home.

I find it here at the misfit table. The instinct to find home is satisfied here.

Daughter, there is nothing heavy about my way. I am a Shepherd to you. I take your sin, your shame, your pain, everything you have. I take it from you and put it upon myself and search for you, and when I find you I joyfully put you on my shoulders and carry you home. We do it together on your interior, as we travel inside my story, heading to our final home—a new city, a banquet, a marriage supper. I show up with a grace that is greater than your sin. Little one, it is all my work so that you can't boast. Your position is rest. Feel the rhythm of the rocking motion while I walk with you, carrying you along. My love, do you see who is doing all the work here? It isn't centered on you. It is centered on me.

fifty-two

It Begins
with Bread

Mary Jo is a praying woman and a ministry leader. She's been a loyal House of Belonging customer for five years. But more than that, she's become my spiritual mother. But only over texting. We have never met in person until I take a trip to Texas where she lives.

⌒⌒

I'm standing in my childhood dream: a kitchen filled with collected china, a pantry filled with vintage linens, cross-stitched towels, aprons on hooks, and metal bins holding cookbooks. A kitchen with a mother who says, "She can give me the little she has." A mother who puts her hands over mine, showing me the "how" of things. Showing me more about how life works rather than what it looks like.

She sits in a chair. I sit and sink back. Tired. Tired from traveling all week. Tired from not feeling family and tired from following breadcrumbs all these years. But mostly, I'm tired from wanting a mother who will bake bread with me and tell me I'm okay. A mother who will tell me she isn't going anywhere. One who will tell me she will give me the little she knows. Add her little to my little. I want something visceral (deep-rooted) to leave my kids. My grandkids. I want them to know how.

Because I know nobody can stay forever. We all cross over eventually. I'm hoping I can have Mary Jo's little to add into mine. Something tangible. Maybe an inheritance. Something that lasts.

Breadcrumbs have led me to a table, Mary Jo's table. I'm longing for a simpler time, a slower pace, and the scent of bread baking in a home and a sense of peace in the moment.

Suddenly, I'm reminded that the mess in my life, the chaos, the stickiness of the dough underneath our fingernails and the aroma of chicken noodle soup simmering on the stove on a cold Friday afternoon means we are not merely alive—we are living—and that is a wonderful thing.

We sit at a table to come together and inherit one another. Inherit one another like a gift. Family.

I watch Mary Jo light a candle and think to myself, *She is four decades deep into adventuring with God, eating breadcrumbs and acting on them.*

I tell her I'm hungry. She smiles, eyes twinkling, and tells me she knows.

"It begins with bread," she answers. She looks me in the eyes and says, "Daughter, let me give you the little I know, okay?"

"Okay," I answer.

For the first time I feel myself being mothered. A mother and daughter, baking in a kitchen. This is family.

"Everything is laid out and ready, dear." She tells me to measure the flour. Four cups. She asks me to put my hands in the flour. "What does it feel like?" she asks.

I slide my hands into the flour. My hands feel the flour's cool airiness. Mixing flour with water creates something living— bread—that satisfies physical hunger. God's Word, married with the Holy Spirit, creates something living, satisfying spiritual hunger.

Next, I mix the wet ingredients with the dry ingredients until Mary Jo says that's good. I turn off the mixer, pull up the hook. Mary Jo asks me what I see. I watch the dough, rough, dull and full of lumps, hanging itself, in need of rescue. *That was me!* I think to myself.

The dough cannot get off the hook by itself; I have to pull it off. All it has to do is let me. I have to let Papa pull me from the bottom of my life, set my feet on new land, and put me back together. I am the lump of dough, my heart needy for kneading. My story, the raw ingredients.

Papa uses my raw ingredients in his story line. I just have to let him.

I hold the dough, letting it rest in my hands. I feel its weight. I lay it gently on the floured surface. Mary Jo shows me how to knead.

"Now it's your turn," she says. I begin kneading.

I imagine I'm the lump of dough in Papa's hands. Resting. Awake in the moment of what it "feels" like to be held. My body relaxes into weightlessness.

Suddenly, I hear the voice I've heard since childhood, "I'm not good at this." It slips out, and Mary Jo hears it. I wish I could take it back. *It sounds weak,* I think to myself. I know it isn't a healthy thought. I know it is a lie.

"Tiff, remember, you are the boss of the dough," Mary Jo tells me. "You tell it what to do."

"I've never been good at bossing anything," I tell Mary Jo, smiling.

"It takes practice, do you hear me?" She winks.

I know it's true. With practice I will get better at bossing dough around. Now that's funny! The dough rests and rises for an hour, then she has me punch it down. We roll, braid, and lay the dough to rest and rise for another two hours.

Mary Jo makes hot tea in china cups, the ones I treasured when I walked in. She says, come, let's go to my prayer room. I quickly learn that what Mary Jo says, I do.

Mary Jo's prayer room feels like mine. Bookcases of Bibles, books, and journals. Containers of colored pencils, markers, pencils, and pens. And candles. And House of Belonging art on almost every wall. All I can think is, *How can someone be so much like you and not be your mother?*

"You sit in my listening chair, okay?"

Seated in her listening chair, I close my eyes and imagine myself as an experienced woman whose heart is at rest in the center of her home, in the midst of chaos, in the middle of her own family.

Little one, let me keep my hands on your heart just like you had yours on your dough. There is a rhythm in my hands, my love. Mixing, kneading, rolling, braiding, and resting to rise.

My heart is learning rest, even in the chaos. Especially in the chaos.

We journal a bit and drink our tea. Mary Jo seems distracted, wrestling. I think she's wrestling with God. About me. I know she wants me to have boundaries in my life. A family. A home to put down roots.

I watch her, memorizing her spirit, her heart, the way God has—and is—shaping her. Not conforming her to this world but conforming her into a cross. I won't forget this day. I wish we would have known each other years ago. I wish I lived by her. I want to throw myself at her feet and tell her to teach me everything she knows. I feel like Ruth. She, my Naomi.

Mary Jo gets up quickly to put the bread in the oven, comes back in telling me we are going to pray. She tells me to close my eyes and hold out my hands. I feel my hands fill with heaviness. I cry as she holds my hands in hers, praying. When she's finished we open our eyes. I open my hands to see tiny black seeds. She explains to me that these are black mustard seeds she brought back from Israel. She's had them for a few years. She didn't know what to do with them, until now. She tells me they are misfits. I tell her they feel weighty. Costly even.

I know it's another breadcrumb. I take and eat.

"The bread is done," Mary Jo says. "Let's head downstairs."

I take the bread out of the oven, set it on the stovetop, and turn around. Then she speaks four words into my heart. "You're a natural, daughter."

I never knew bones could ache for words as simple as these.

No longer is my family lineage only my earthly mother, grandmother, and great-grandmother. Now I sit with my spiritual mothers. I smile, imagining myself sitting with Sarah as she gets three cups of her best flour, kneads it, and makes bread for Abraham and God.

I come from a long story line of misfit women who took God at his word because they had no other option: women like Sarah, Ruth, Jael, Deborah, Rahab, Esther, Mary, the Samaritan woman, the Canaanite woman, Martha, and Miriam, to name a few.

And now Mary Jo. She's a misfit too.

If they can do it, so can I! Here, I fit. In these story lines, I belong. This feels like home. Like family. Eating the bread. Eating the words. Praying the Word. Sharing what God is doing in our lives. Together.

There is something in baking bread and setting tables. To be in the center of our home might be the most powerful missional weapon today, our homes becoming lighthouses for the hungry—stomach hungry *and* heart hungry.

I'm a misfit, Papa. I don't need to belong to my culture. I belong to Jesus, to his kingdom. I see it now. I have no other option than to take you at your word. I will go and bake bread and set misfit tables. First for me, then for others. I say yes. I sit and rest and listen to you. I'll teach others to sit and rest and listen too. I'll do more than follow the breadcrumbs. I'll eat them. I'll feed them to others too.

It begins with breadcrumbs, the Holy Spirit, and yeses. It begins with bread. It begins with me.

My hands are always at work and play in your life, kneading more of me into your heart, cutting away what hurts. Let me pull you up. Let me. Receive from me. This is hard for you, little one.

There is something in baking
bread and setting tables. To be
in the center of our home might
be the most powerful missional
weapon today, our homes becoming
lighthouses for the hungry—
stomach hungry
& heart hungry.
—Papa

My love and gifts have no strings. It doesn't take what you don't want to give. It will not look like the world's love. My love is simple. Simple but strong. It doesn't coerce you, but it will cost you everything you have, cost you everything you think you need.

I enjoy you so much. All I want to do is spend the rest of your life being your first love. Let me keep being your food. Keep on eating of me. I never run out; there is always more. Let me be what satisfies your hunger. Keep writing our love story. It will be the best love story you've ever written. I keep my promises, little one. Try me and see.

fifty-three

Jesus Eats with Everyone

I open my Bible and journal and date the top of the page. I'm sitting at my table, made from an old house in Lebanon, Tennessee, that my friends Rick and Craig made. I imagine the untold stories inside her. I rub my hand over scuffs, over little Etta's name in black permanent marker. I notice that corners that were once flush no longer meet. A glass vase holds center stage, carrying a single purple hydrangea bloom that holds to its last bit of life. It will die giving something beautiful to the world. I think about it, take a sip of coffee gone cold.

If my table told my story today, what would it say? My table would say it is a sort of triage church, a safe space to share my broken and hurting heart with others, to share how Christ gave me gospel-medicine, and to share how God can heal those who gather with me. It would say that God can fix us together, knot us together, like nets. When cast out into the deep water of life, we can pull people to safety.

My table would say it's becoming an ancient table of fellowship and not just a place of entertainment. My table will be a boat, a lifeboat, pulling the shipwrecked up out of the water.

Or maybe my tables would gather together and tell the stories of how they've moved from trailer to trailer, house to house. My new table would share how it's become the place for a sort of movable feast. I take it wherever I go. Everyone I meet a potential guest. To feed. To receive. To eat, together.

I look at the table, and now I'm telling a story. The table could be an inheritance, something I leave my kids and my kids' kids, an invitation to remember God's faithfulness, his provision, his desire to meet with his people in the land of the living.

My mind keeps spinning as I write in my journal. *Time is robbing and cheating us, Papa.* Hurry, fears, and scarcity are tearing us away from the table, devouring families, tearing them apart. And we're letting them.

My family has been torn apart, still tattered in many places. What's the remedy? Can we build our lives on table fellowship? Turn tables into heart-hospitals at the center of every home? Can we make them biblical tables, places for God's Word? God's Word, food, table, and people? Love and forgiveness the cement that binds us together?

There is a nurturing wholeness in God's words, and when we take and eat, they go straight to our hearts and to the hearts of people gathered at the table. We give those words away as God-stories around tables in homes. We give them away in all kinds of homes—trailers in the trailer parks, mansions on high hills, cookie-cutter homes in the suburbs. We carry the table with us into the world too. Out into the dark places that hurt, behind the closed, locked doors. The playground, the storm shelters, the prisons, and the community spaces. We see behind smiles, look-goods, and do-goods.

I write more thoughts, and as I consider that this table is for everyone, I'm hungry to do something I've never done before. What would it look like if I set the table and invited everyone who has ever hurt me? What would it be like to sit with them at a table that wouldn't turn? A table that is safe. A table where I can be okay in my naked skin. No secret keeping. No hiding. A table where the forgiving, healing, loving Jesus is present. A table of reconciliation. A table of forgiveness. A table where we earnestly assess generational sins, habits, and patterns, to lay them out and navigate them together.

I think about those who've wronged me. Oppressed me. Held me captive. Abused me. Betrayed me. Cheated on me. Left me to struggle. Left me to defend myself. Broken me. Pushed me down. Didn't listen to my nos. Deceived me. Didn't mother me. Father me. Friend me.

But I remember the God who has never left me. Who's stuck with me. Listened to me. Spoken to me. Nurtured me. Held me.

Because I know now that the something-more I need, we all need, is a deep resting on the gospel of transforming grace. That God is the Rescuer. This grace isn't to be shored up in my own powers. No. This grace is my daily minute-by-minute, take-as-often-as-needed prescription. As I open my mouth, the Rescuer spoon-feeds my faith.

I'll go with you, Papa says, so I pull up a chair in my mind and close my eyes. I imagine those who've hurt me at that table.

I imagine Jesus there too. I watch as he walks around the table. I watch him place his hands on their hearts. One on the front and one on the back, as if he is holding a book, their heart-story. He is the only one who can hold a human story, especially a story of someone who abuses his people. It can't break him anymore.

I watch his face as he leans down, into their story. It is the kindest face I have ever seen. His kindness runs so deep. I hear him whisper to each person:

"Open your heart to me. Give me your heart. Give me your guilt, your shame, your superiority over other people, your arrogance, blindness, coldness of heart, your abuse, your moral strength, despair, and your fear, little one. I love you as you are right now. Let me pick you up, bring you back home. Let me give you my heart for yours. Let me give you liberty and belonging. Let me help you follow the map back home, set you on your feet on the greatest adventure, stand you up in your name, give you freedom right here at the table. I see someone I love. I have so much to give you. Let me give you a new way to see yourself. A new mirror. Let me show you the way Papa sees you."

I look around the table. Some faces remain the same, others soften, and others cry.

In this moment, I watch love do its work. I see the hearts of those who've hurt me through the lens of their story, not my own. I see them through the lens of them as a child, how they suffered their own pains. Their own abuses. Their own traumas. Their own hand-me-down sin patterns from their parents. They didn't get to choose that. But God knows them. He knows their hearts. He knows where to find each of us.

I see it now, Papa. You're working. Now I see a bit more how we can love our enemies—the same way you do. I'm understanding a bit more how grace works powerfully in my own life when I forgive. Writing my story, I see my own heart, your forgiveness. You prepare a table for us in the middle of our enemies, and you join us there. You tend to our enemies. You bring healing.

Oh, Papa! I can't stop gazing at your hands working on hearts. I see the love in your eyes for them too. At your table there are no favorites. I knew that in my head. Now I see with my heart. I want to live that way too!

I watch and watch, and then I see me too. I've been the abuser, liar, and cheater. I've been the oppressor, the Pharisee. I was the mother who abandoned her children and divorced her husband. I'm sick with guilt and shame. Pride and unbelief too. My sin has hurt others. My sin has brought chaos, sin that has separated. Sin that has killed, stolen, and destroyed. *But the gospel, Papa!*

And then I see her. She's sitting next to me, looking down, wringing her hands. She looks familiar.

I lean closer and whisper, "Hey!"

She looks up and my breath catches. I'm looking into my child-hood face. The version of me that is eight, and she is holding a small white box. My offering. It was all I had. I sense her wanting to let everything go. Once and for all.

"But it's all of everything I have," she whispers, her lip quivering. I watch Papa's hand lift her chin up to him, face to face. He bends down, cups her face, wipes her tears, pushing her hair back so he can look her in the eyes. He speaks straight to her.

"Little one, don't look down. Look up here. At me. You don't need to fix yourself up or get yourself together. Just come and sit. Take and eat.

"My words do the work of putting back together. It's a table of transforming grace. The light is always on. I am always home. When you feel the weight of the world, come. When you are busting loose with joy, come. Tell me all of everything, little one. I want to hear. I'm here. I'm unchangeable. I'm here to take the hits for you. To cover your sin. Forgive you. Help you up. Help you stand. Help you navigate. I want to be your first meal. Your every meal. My words, fresh, daily provision from morning till night and in all the in-between hours.

"Little one, my table is an altar.

"I take your little white box with all of everything you have and exchange it. If you give me your sin, I give you back a holy life. Every day, this exchange is open to you."

I lean over, wrapping my arms around her, cheek to cheek, wallpapering her soul to mine.

This table is for somebodies. Jesus turns to both of us, and he says he makes everyone into a somebody. And together we both know: we are seen, known, and loved by our first love. Our God. Our Papa.

I pull back, looking at her. I tell her how much I love her. I tell her she's okay now. That she's been found. She knows the direction she's going. She does know what to do. I tell her Jesus is our Shepherd now. He has never lost the way. How I love who she is becoming. I tell her everything I've learned so far. We talk for what seems like hours at the table. We go back through the stories everyone wrote into our lives. The ones that squeezed the music out of us. I tell her I've been living in her shoes, but I'm not eight anymore. The shoes don't fit anymore. They haven't in a very long time.

I tell her to look at the table. I tell her there is the best meal waiting. She doesn't have to live in starvation anymore. Taking care of herself. Shoring up things, just in case. I tell her we always have a home and a meal. I tell her we aren't slaves anymore. We are daughters. There is no more clutching things and people as if that is all we have. Now there is a rest, a rhythm—baking bread, dropping breadcrumbs, and setting tables.

At the table, I can see it now. Jesus saves, heals, and keeps hearts. Jesus helps. He doesn't get dirty by touching our mess, whatever that mess may be. He's not afraid of abusers, liars, or cheaters either. He comes into any dirty house, eats with all the misfits in it, and makes that house clean.

I know my relationships won't all be restored. Sometimes they can't be. Either way, the table is a safe place, a place of healing for me, my friends, and my enemies. A place to eat the Word together.

I open my eyes, still sitting at my barnwood table.

I'm not a Papa of chaos or confusion. I come in to help you put your life back in order. To give it a foundation that can no longer be shaken down. A structure to hold you up. I give you my salvation. Give me your imperfect record, and I'll give you my righteousness. Give me all of your everything, and I'll give you mine. For you, Jesus made this exchange once and for all on the cross. Then, day after day, we remember it and continue it at my table. You see? The table is an altar of exchange: you give me your mess; I feed you my messianic meal.

This is our new daily rhythm. It will look nothing like it did before. You will look nothing like before. And as we travel through the world, we will break off breadcrumbs for others. These bread-crumbs will leave a trail, a freedom trail. They will tell others that true belonging is with me. They will show a way back home to my heart.

My heart aches for my family. I want my family back.

It's simple, really. I gave everything to get you back. To receive me it will cost you everything you have, and yet, as you take and eat every day at my table, I will give you everything that I am. Jesus says, this is my body, this is my bread, broken for you—broken for family. There is nothing I want more than families to be put back together.

Join me as my warrior daughter. Let me use your voice as I made it, a battle cry, a dinner bell, to call others to turn around, come back home. Come to the real table, the ancient table. Let me recover what is lost. Let me repair what is broken. Let me restore what is not there.

Taste me and see.

The table is
an altar of
exchange:
you give me
your mess;
I feed you
my messianic
meal.
—Papa

Family of Misfits

I close my eyes and see myself standing in the doorway of a framed house. A house of belonging. I searched for this house for years, thinking I'd find it with my mom, my grandma, or some man. I used to think it was a house in the real world, even though it might be a church or some house God would build. Now I know the house Papa wanted to build is inside me. It's a place for the two of us.

I run my hand over the wood of the doorframe, wondering what color of door she will have when it's all finished. I look at the stone slab and see "Come as you are" etched in that stone. My welcome mat.

Sunlight streams in from all sides. There are no walls yet, and I realize I am this house. I'm an exposed frame. Bones with no skin. Still being finished. Still, I smile.

"Excuse me," a voice interrupts my reverie. "She's been torn down to bare bones. The framing is done. She's sturdy now. Foundation is good. She's ready," the Carpenter says. He says he's restoring order and beauty. He's the structure. He unrolls the plans. Runs his finger over each room. Asks me where I want to start. I tell him the dining room. I want to set up my table, a place for the two of us, for others. I leave him to his paper and figuring, and I head back to the front porch.

He's making me into a temple. In the middle of that temple, he's placing a table for us. I can't stop smiling.

I see now how love has pulled me to Papa's table time after time, day after day. It's where he whispers promises to me, where he bandages my wounds, where he feeds me. And because I've hungered and thirsted for love, for healing, and for food for what feels like most of my life, the table has become our place, the place for my "misfittedness" in a house of belonging. I can trust him with what happens with my business, my family, my health, my story that hangs in midair. Where I live or don't live doesn't matter. As long as I have my hunger, my voice, and my pen, I'm going to come to the table. Every single day. Take and eat. Invite others. Show and tell the gospel meal. Share my God-story.

There are so many who've experienced the love of God at tables just like this. I've met them. We have the only cure—the gospel. It puts us back together again. We gather around Papa's Word, around tables with food, telling our God-stories. We've come to know the only table that transforms is the table where Jesus sits. And Jesus's table is where the wounded, wild and raw, are welcomed. It is here the hungry misfits can pull up a chair, have the best meal they've ever tasted, and walk away full. So full, in fact, you'd want even your worst enemy to experience that kind of fullness. So full you'll want to forgive. So full you'd want to give up everything, and I mean everything, and follow Jesus to the table every day, every chance you get. It's the only table that can put anyone together again. Even broken families. Especially families.

Will you come? Will you join this family of misfits? We've saved a place for you, a place where we hear Papa's song every day.

Little one, you will always be a misfit in this world when you eat Jesus's body and drink his blood, when you remember true freedom is a radical thing that comes at great cost. My freedom is a gift that comes through pain. A gift that is free. Receive it. Let it fill you. Then give it away. Then you will taste true freedom. True peace. True belonging. True home.

HOUSE OF BELONGING

WWW.THEHOUSEOFBELONGING.COM

@HOUSEOFBELONGING

HOUSE OF BELONGING® ✝
MISFIT TABLE
GOOD NEWSPAPER

WORD.   FOOD.   STORY.

Will you come? Will you join this family of misfits? We've saved a place for you. A place where we hear Papa's song every day. We've come to know that the only table that transforms is the table where Jesus sits. And Jesus' table is where the wounded, wild and raw are welcomed. It is here the hungry misfits can pull up a chair, have the best meal they've ever tasted, and walk away full. So full, in fact, you'd want even your worst enemy to experience this kind of fullness.

Join the Misfit Community by scanning the QR code below or visiting misfittable.com.

WE ARE MISFITS A PEOPLE WHO TAKE GOD AT HIS WORD RISK-TAKERS LIGHT-BRINGERS GAME-CHANGERS GENERATIONAL WRECKING BALLS HOME-BUILDERS WORLD-TRAVELERS YES SAYERS RED SEA WALKERS KINGDOM OF DARKNESS TOPPLERS WE REFUSE TO GIVE UP IN OR OUT WE ARE AUDACIOUS PIONEERS WHO FORGE NEW WAYS WE ARE REBELS WITH THE GOSPEL WHO GO OUTSIDE OF RELIGION WHERE JESUS IS FACILITATING RESTORATION AND SETTING TABLES THE INSIDER WORLD IS NOT OUR HOME PULL UP A CHAIR WE ARE MISFITS A PEOPLE WHO TAKE GOD AT HIS WORD

HOUSE OF BELONGING